Hodgepodge

~ REVISITED ~

Debby Arthur Warner

ISBN: 978-1-7349415-5-5

Library of Congress Control Number: 2026913466

First edition
Printed in the United States of America

Cover and text design by Laurie Goralka Design

For more information:
gjauthor@gmail.com
www.debbyarthurwarner.com

Table of Contents

Poetry

Children's Section

Short Stories & Memoirs

Freeda

Introduction

I first wrote *Hodgepodge* in 2022, mainly for my family and a few close friends. Although it was unedited, I wanted to publish "as is" to give a glimpse into my process, and to leave them with a collection of my other projects in addition to my novels. I also included some very personal thoughts and poetry, some of which have been removed in this version.

Among the poetry, children's stories, and short stories, you will find glimpses into my life. This is a collection of fiction with spurts of nonfiction in the mix. While I've removed several writings from the first version, I've added more new work in *Hodgepodge Revisited*. My favorite story to work on was "Freeda," a mini bio about an amazing woman who, in a few short years, will become a centenarian.

I hope that something will resonate with you within this collection of *Hodgepodge Revisited* . . . either on an emotional, spiritual, or amusing level.

Acknowledgments

I am tremendously grateful for the professional individuals that I've been blessed to work with.

Content Editor—Carole London

Line Editor—Bonnie Beach

Proofreader—Linda Munson-Haley

Graphic Designer—Laurie Casselberry

I appreciate their knowledge and expertise in the publishing industry.

Freeda, you truly are amazing! Thank you for showing me how exciting each day can be when you continue doing what you've always loved to do—and never allow age to have the upper hand.

Whether you'll be sitting at the bar in Texas Roadhouse with your friends or dancing the night away at the Moose, I know when heaven calls, you'll be smiling and bringing with you an energy that those who've gone before have never seen. But until that day comes, I look forward to enjoying many more interesting and exciting years with you.

POETRY

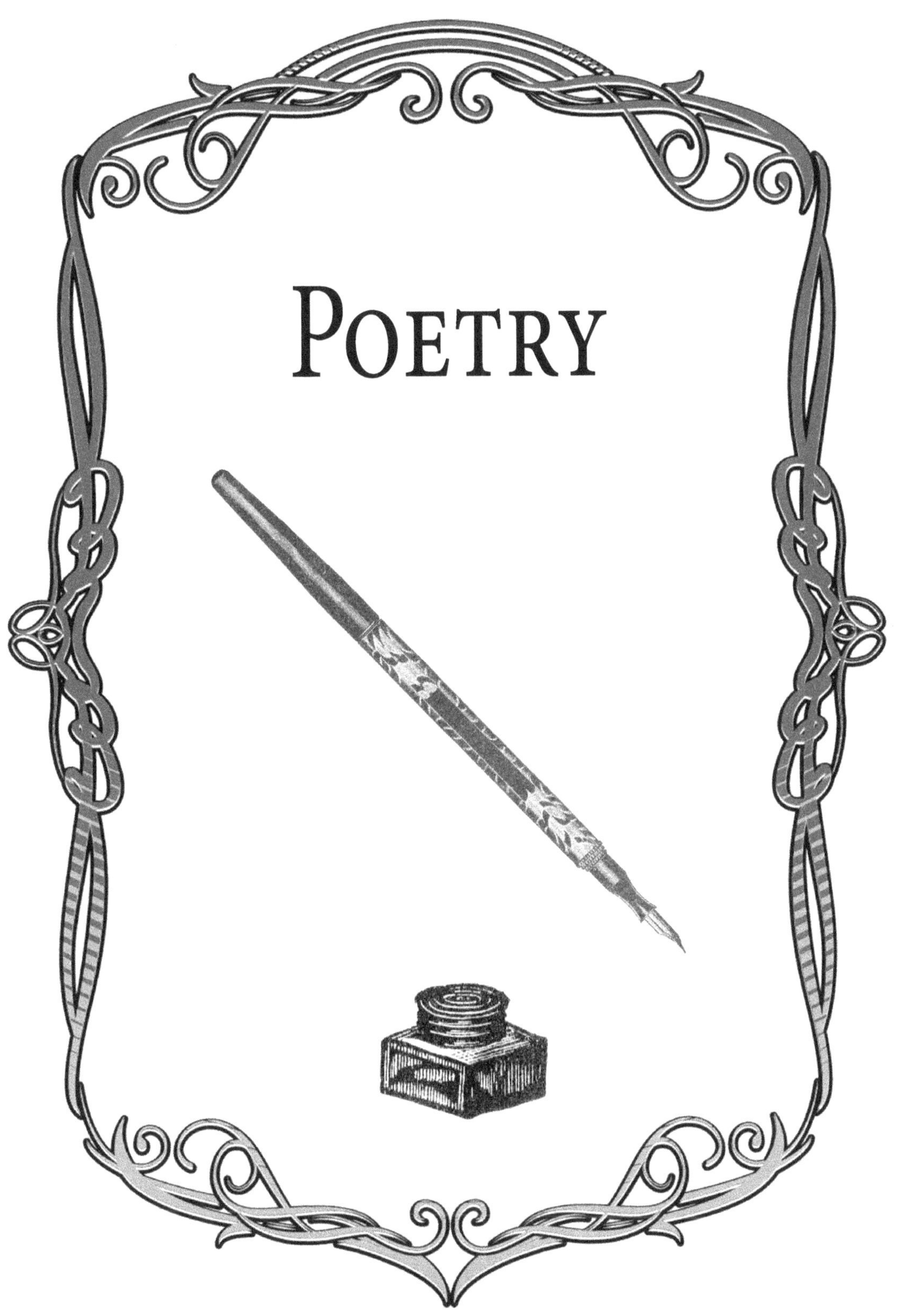

Moonlit Night

I stare upon a moonlit night
In awe, in wonder of its sight
Could man have truly landed there
And walked its ground without a care?

The sky is full, the stars are bright
And I'm beneath a moonlit night

A tranquil evening, no clouds to despair
Quiet serenity awaits me here
Distractions are nil, I refuse to allow
Not even the sound from a common hoot owl

The days are full, no end in sight
But I breathe deep upon a moonlit night

Impressed with Mountains High

I've been impressed with mountains high
Carved statuesque reaching toward the sky
And rugged edges surpassing the timbers wide

I've been intrigued with those on foot
Climbing thousands of feet with weighted backs
In search of the wondrous elusive look

I've seen the views both near and far
From coast to coast and Midwest regions
And mostly traveled with my car

The awesome Rockies standing tall
Inspire tourists and photos plenty
But most picturesque are the Smokies in Fall

The reds, the oranges, the yellowish hues
I've been impressed with mountains high

Peaceful and Spirited Sea

Lure of the sea
Calls me back
To the serenity I feel
Observing its timeless beauty

Peaceful and spirited sea
You inspire me
With your vast mass
Of endlessness

Fresh salty air
Beckons thoughts and memories
To be written
From my balcony

Peaceful and spirited sea
You inspire me

Sense of Presence

The spirit lingers
Long after death
Comforting loved ones
Left behind
Eventually
It too will leave

Sense of presence
Dwindling, fading
Only memories
Remain

LUNCH ALONE

I went to lunch today
By myself
I sat outside in nature
Listened to the birds singing
Admired the beautiful spring flowers

I do this a lot,
Eat alone
Not by choice
But circumstance
I don't mind, really
I'm getting used to it

There are advantages
Having lunch alone
I can eat without talking
Finish my meal
Before it gets cold

Strange what you can do
When you know
It's better than not doing

FURRY FRIENDS

Furry creatures of mine
Snuggled closely
Next to me
No will to move
No sense of time

Passively sleeping
On their sides
Dreamworld calm
Blissfully serene
Furry creatures of mine

WIND

The wind carries everything away
If only that were true
I'd release all the worries
Of the day
To the wind at night
Wake up in the morning
Without a care

No mourning friends
Who've lost loved ones
No concerns for family
With life-threatening illnesses
No fear for grandchildren
Of motherless households
No need to worry
The wind has carried everything away

A fresh new day
The phone rings
Then rings again
One concern after another
If only the wind
Would carry it all away

NUTSHELLS

The spring has sprung
The bed is done
Cannot sleep
And so, I tweet

Dirty dishes piled high
Dishwasher groaning
No room inside
I think it will die

I come before you
With lots of hope
Oh, never mind
It was only a joke

I sit here weary
The day is done
I can't remember
If I had any fun

Two shakes of salt
One of pepper
It looked good
But tasted like leather

Birds are singing
Trees are swinging
Ring-a-ding-ding
It must be spring

I stepped on the scale
It lied again
Said I gained weight
Threw it in the lake

Handmade Teddy Bear

He sits on the sofa
Wearing your glasses
Clothed in your shirt

I look at him
And smile
I loved that shirt
You wore

It feels different now
Empty, still,
No life inside

I know this
Yet he gives me
Comfort

That handmade teddy bear
Sitting there
Wearing your shirt
And glasses

WALKING IN ASPEN

I walked to clear my head
Down the street and by the park
National prayer day, the sign said
But few were seated there

Down the street and by the park
I went around to the other side
But few were seated there
The meat and cheese shop straight ahead

I went around to the other side
National prayer day the sign said
The meat and cheese shop straight ahead
I walked to clear my head

THE COUPLE

Walking side by side
They still hold hands
And smile when they
Glance each other's way

Is it love, comfort,
Or convenience that keeps
Them together now
Or years of history
They can't bear to relive alone

They stare straight ahead
She points out a bird
Searching for a crumb
He nods and reaches in his pocket
And finds a saltine cracker
Left over from lunch

By the time he gets it opened
The bird has left
But he throws the crumbled-up
Cracker anyway, and waits

Nothing happens
He smiles and reaches for her hand
They continue their walk

Side by side
Hand in hand
Together

RUMBLES OF THE WAVES

In the rumbles of the waves
I listen to its voice

My mind is calm
Allowing the ocean to speak
Memories flood forth
Illuminating what's to be seen

A love treasured
A life well lived
No regrets

Gratitude for what was
Accepting what is
Letting go of yesterday

Thankful for the rumbles of the waves
Allowing the ocean to speak

THE DREAM

It's in my mind
I see it clear
But when I wake
It isn't there

All through the day
There is no threat
I'm at peace
My dream is at rest

But when the moon
Comes out at night
A peaceful dream
Turns into fright

It's in my mind
I see it clear
But when I wake
It isn't there

SLEEPLESS NIGHT

When I awakened
It was the middle of the night
Not the morning I anticipated
With its welcoming light

Should I get up
I asked myself, looking at the clock
3 AM is not the time to rise
Close your eyes
Give sleep another try

As I lay there peacefully
Restful and still
Waiting for slumber to lull me
Back into its comforting arms
An alarm went off
Inside my head
Something must be wrong it said

Then like an unwanted tornado
In the wee hours of morning
Anxious thoughts appeared
Out of nowhere
No longer was my mind
Peaceful and clear

Jumping out of bed
I reached for my phone
But who would I call
With unfounded thoughts
Of my own

Hospitals, police stations
Seemed like a good place to start
Nothing made sense
My worries continued to soar
I had to do something
Take control before
These runaway fears
Gave way to
Uncontrollable tears

Taking a few deep breaths
I grabbed a pencil and pad
Sat in the recliner and
Began writing my concerns

I wrote and wrote
Until I felt lighter
The exact moment I drifted off
Is unclear

But I awoke
To a bright sunny morning
Restful and calm
My once restless night
No longer in sight

SNOW

Blustery, wintery
Devilish snow
Creating havoc on
Innocence below

Swirling, turning
Covering up
All that's in sight
And some that is not

What is your purpose
I wonder and frown
Yet in awe of your
Beauty and all it surrounds

Snow angels, sledding,
Snowmen to build
Give children of all
Ages a wonderful thrill

Caution is preached by
Those in the know
For anyone daring
To be on the road

Drifts are aplenty
But heed my advice
Never hide in one
You may not survive

The mountains are calling
Skiers to come
Promising hillsides of
Powder and fun
Not all are appreciative
Of the white chilly dust
But for winter enthusiasts
It's definitely a must.

Spring

The snow is leaving
Making room for spring blossoms
And new life begins

Birds on tree limbs chirp
Grass wakens from winter's rest
Lovers roam the park

Tulips show their buds
Robins search the ground for worms
Sprinklers water lawns

Air smells freshly sweet
Neighbors occupy porches
Barbecues in sight

Together Again

Our souls will meet
I know not when
But this I know
We'll be together again

The cold of winter
Sees little warmth
Resembling the time
We spend here on earth

It seems an eternity
From birth until death
But time spent here
Is a split second at best

When we must leave
Heaven welcomes us in
Joining family and friends
Forever without end

Nothing to Say

I took a walk the other day
Alone, by myself, and
I wanted it that way

I passed a woman
She said hi, I politely replied hello
Nothing more was said, and
I wanted it that way
I had nothing more to say

REFLECTIONS

She feels ancient now
In her third trimester of life
Memories of homecoming queen
Youth, vitality, beauty,
Recessed in the past.

The mirror reflects a stranger
Loose skin, puffy eyes, wrinkles.
Gray hair if not colored.

When did her spirit leave?
Was it after the divorce?
When Mama died?
Daughter's endless needs?
Or after death invaded
The other side of her bed?

Caregiving has taken its toll
Existing is difficult
Cries go unheard
Heart-breaking-unfelt
No one's there
To hear, to feel, to care,
To help her move forward
Help her redefine who she is.

Hold her, cry with her
Show her she's worthy
Needed, wanted, and loved

Is it a wonder she feels ancient
Beaten, worn down
Not interested that she might
Have many more sunrises
Before her final sunset?

Prompt:
Write a 26-line poem using all of the alphabet where the first line starts with "A,"
the second "B," the third "C," etc., and the final line "Z".

THE MIGHTY TORNADO

Again, the wind blows
But this time it's different
Controlled as if in charge
Devastating to watch
Eerie, when you think about it
Forging ahead without discriminating
Gaining momentum when it wants
Harnessing debris along the way
Insensitive to who may get hurt
Jumping around as if on stilts
Keeping focused so not to let up
Laughing and throwing things in the air
Mocking mortals running for cover
Not caring whether buildings are destroyed
Or that the very young are injured
Purposely striking everything in its path
Quaking not at all the destruction
Relishing in the damage left behind
Sulking, only because it's over
Time to disappear for now
Understanding its demise is near
Vanishing as quickly as it appeared
Weakened to a memory
Xenophobia, animosity waning
Yearning for what was
Zealous no more

Try to Imagine

I try to imagine what it was like.
Euphoria carried you for months at a time,
You seemed larger than life.
Then the anger, rage, and depression.
Was this the mom who took us to the beach?
And sat with a friend on the boardwalk,
Laughing the day away?

I try to imagine what it was like.
I thought you were beautiful, friendly, and proud
When you appeared in my second-grade class.
The kids laughed and made fun,
Too much perfume, too much makeup,
They said you smelled like a stink bomb
And looked like a clown.
I cried.
The teacher hugged me and
Said those things weren't true,
She thought you were beautiful, too.

I try to imagine what it was like,
When you worked late into the night
And we kids were left alone
And dad was not at home.
We were scared,
We were hungry.
You brought back leftovers from the café
They were old
They were cold.

I try to imagine what it was like.
Dad moved us south to start anew
I was sad, and so were you.
You found work,
I attended high school.
I was from the North
The South never forgot
I wasn't a rebel, I didn't fit in
My father wasn't a doctor or lawyer
I had no friends.

I try to imagine what it was like
To struggle all your life,
Only to be in the have-nots.
To have the grandiose illusions you could do more
Buy out the store
Not realizing you were poor.
Falling into the depths of despair
When the bills would arrive
And you'd pretend they weren't there.

I try to imagine what it was like.
We were married and
Away from your life.
You had no time before,
But now you wanted to see us more.
You felt depressed when
We didn't show.
It seemed we were always on the go.

Continued

I try to imagine what it was like.
You became my best friend.
I loved you more than life.
And we'd always phone
To say, I love you, good night.
You felt unworthy
You felt humbled.
For many years you seemed all right
But soon the demons
Had you in sight.

I try to imagine what it was like.
You succumbed to the darkness
I wanted you to fight.
The twisted serpents
Invaded your mind.
It didn't matter that I was there,
That I cared.
You were elsewhere.

I try to imagine what it was like.
You emerge from the depths
Of the bottomless pit.
You're flying high
Toward the sky.
I am confused,
Either way I lose.
I can't confine you
Can't contain you,
Am I the one losing my mind?

I try to imagine what it was like.

GROCERY LIST

I'm confused
I must admit
Walked out the door
Without my list

As I wander
Through the store
Wants come easy
Needs don't recall

Ice cream, cookies, potato chips
Not much healthy
In the mix
Wasn't on my grocery list

Roasted chicken
That will do
Add some rice
Carrots, too
Cart is full
Time to go

Home again
I'm relieved
Bought everything
That I need
Plus twenty more
I should have missed
Wasn't on my grocery list

FAMILY VACATION

Ups and downs
Perks and quirks
Such is the life
Of the family vacation

Sorting and packing
Loading unloading
Settling in
Fun now begins

Beds are chosen
Dinner is made
Who cleans up?
There isn't a maid

Gather on the balcony
Catch up on life
Each shares a tale
Both small and tall
But who's to say
If it happened at all

Morning comes early
Nighttime amiss
Sleepy eyes waken
So much to do
Miniature golf, swimming
Horseback riding, too

Shopping, hiking
Grandma stays back
Time for her
To take a nap

All too soon
It comes to an end
Kids grab a snack
Car's all packed
Time to go home

Unload and sort
Put everything away
Not as much fun
As a week ago today

Ahh, the family vacation

THE WILLOWS

Through the willows
I hear your voice
Though I know you're not there.
When I sit by the river
The water whispers
Familiar sounds
As it breaks gently
Against the rocks.

I breathe in the sweet
Scent of spring flowers
Swaying in the meadows
Hummingbirds search for nectar
Butterflies flutter freely
Beautiful scenes
Etched in my memory

SILENCE

Walk along with me
In silence
Feel the breeze
Upon your face

Listen to the rhythm
Of leaves
Swaying through
The aspens

Allow the music
Of singing birds
To be heard

With all your senses
Absorb nature
Lose yourself
In the moment

In silence

REMNANTS OF TIME

I feel the remnants of time
Little spurts here and there
Of years gone by
Sometimes I wish
I could grab the memory
Hold it dear to my heart
Enjoy every moment
Of the experiences
I had back then
Does nostalgia make it
Feel more meaningful now
Because I'm older and
Can't play with
My childhood friend
Spend summers with
My cousins
Watch my children grow?
If only I had known
How quickly it would pass

WEATHER

What matters
Don't know
Maybe rain
Not snow
Sunny skies
Nice surprise

Wind no
Couldn't last
Eyes burn
Hair flies
Nose runs
Go inside

Rain's okay
Sometimes snow
Sunny skies
Perfect day
Wind no
Go away

IMAGINED MAYBE?

I came
I saw
Was concerned
Went home
Got friend
Off again
She looked
Nothing there
So left
I'm alone
Imagined maybe?

Walked away
Blinked eyes
Looked back
Something moved
Shaking bush
Must see
Shouldn't have
Now flee
Don't tell
Who'd believe
Imagined maybe?

NATURE

Mountains high
Valleys low

Meadows flourish
Flowers grow

Deserts dry
Cactus thrive

Pastures plenty
Cows survive

Children's Section

Hippity Hop

Hippity hop
Bunny just flopped
On his back
He looks quite flat
Rolls to his side
Lets out a sigh
Up again
Off again
Hippity hop

Raindrops

A raindrop fell
On my head today
I said go away
I want to play

Then another came
And did the same

More and more
It began to pour
I wanted to play
I went out anyway

I'M ONLY TEN

I'm big
I'm gawky
I'm only ten
I am what I am
Said Tom
To his friend

ICE CREAM

Vanilla, strawberry
Chocolate, too
So many flavors
How can I choose?

Have some fun
Close your eyes
Spin around
Point to one

Firefly

Joey runs
To catch the light
The sky is full
So many in flight
Easy to catch
The jar has plenty

Watch them glow
Enjoy the show
But don't forget
To let them go

Secret

I'd like to share a secret
I heard the other day
But if it's a secret
I shouldn't give it away

If I tell you what I know
Would you keep it to yourself
Or run like wild horses
And spill it to everyone else?

A secret is a secret
And should be kept that way
Unless it could be harmful
Then you should give it away

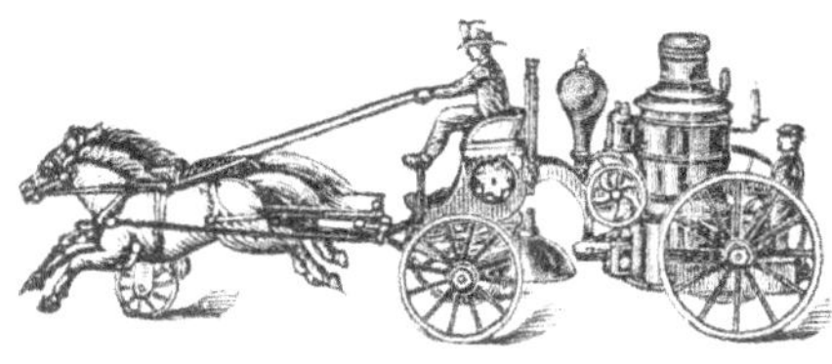

Fire Engine #53

It was red
It was big
It was coming
Down the street

I took a peek
Yelled with glee
When I saw
Fire engine #53

I ran to the curb
Waved my hands
Mr. Jack nodded
And waved back at me

When I grow up
I want to be
A fireman like Mr. Jack
Driving fire engine #53

JIBBER JABBER
THE GABBY TURKEY

Jibber Jabber was his name
Gabbing was his claim to fame
He lived at 21 Turkey Lane
With a family who thought he would
Surely drive them insane.

He was loud, he was boisterous
He wanted to be heard
But no one else could get in a word

The Hildebrans liked him at first
Buying him from a man they had just met at
church

They were told Jibber Jabber liked to boast
That he would make the best
Thanksgiving roast
Giving those at the table
A cause to toast

He knew all turkeys were meant
For a reason
And he wanted to be
The best of the season

There was just one problem
Having him around
They couldn't shut up
That awful sound

He didn't just gobble
Like all of his friends
He squawked and screeched
Scaring off the Hildebran hens

With only a few days left
Before the big meal
It wouldn't be long before their ears
Could begin to heal

It was quiet, it was still
It was the middle of the night
When they wakened startled
By a terrible sight

Jibber Jabber was at the
Foot of the bed
Flapping his wings yelling
From the top of his head

Get out! Get out of the house!
Call the fire department
There's a flame in the shed
Hurry! Hurry! Did you hear what I said?

The Hildebrans scrambled
And ran out the door

Soon the engines arrived
And the fire was put out
All were encouraged to return inside
Which they did with a big thankful sigh

Continued

The shed was saved
And so was the house
No one got hurt
But where was that yakking
turkey
Who sounded the alert?

Jibber Jabber was gone
He was nowhere in sight
Had he seized this moment
To take flight?

They looked upstairs
They looked down
But he was nowhere
To be found

The Hildebrans gathered
And hung their heads
Worried that Jibber Jabber
Might be dead

All of a sudden
The front door burst open
In came Jibber Jabber
Carrying a token

A huge bass he caught
Down at the lake
Explaining how his fish
Would be delicious once baked

They all gave thanks for
Thanksgiving that year
Especially Jibber Jabber
His life had been spared

The Dog in The Boot

The dog in the boot just wanted to play, but others didn't see it that way.
They thought he was mischievous, trouble if you will, because wherever he
went it didn't go well.

Mary and John were playing in their yard when the dog in the boot
happened along.
"Can I play with you?" he asked. "I can be a lot of fun."

Mary shuddered thinking what her mother would say,
so she pleaded with him to go away.

"Why must I go?" Moaned the dog in the boot. "You haven't given me a
chance to show you what I can do. Do you like magic? I'll show you some
great tricks, and I can tell jokes that will make your sides split."

He took three steps closer, then John put up his hand. "Stop where you are
and go away. Mother warned us never to play with
unknown friends on a clear day."

"Hush hush, no need to make a fuss. I won't stay if you don't want to play."
He hung his head and turned his boot around, and Mary noticed a tear
rolling down.

"Wait wait, I'm sure you're very nice, but we have rules and must obey
Mother's advice."

The dog in the boot wiped his face with his paw, reached down in his boot
and pulled out a huge straw. Mary and John were surprised by its size and
asked him to explain how it was hidden inside.

Continued

"This is a magic boot and it holds more than you know. Have a seat on the ground and I'll put on a show."

John and Mary gave a sigh and looked toward the house. They knew they should go inside and hide like a mouse. But the dog in the boot looked harmless enough and they were very curious to see all his stuff. They did as he asked and sat on the ground. Mary could hardly wail to see what was found in that boot now dancing around.

The dog in the boot paused, then slowly reached down and pulled out a huge banner that fell to the ground. Mary counted 50 elephants all in a row, and all but one didn't have toes. Then just as quickly a giant American flag appeared displaying stars so bright it made their eyes tear.

John cried with a plea, "Turn it off, turn it off, or our mother will see!"

"Don't worry, don't worry, your mother won't look," then he pulled out a computer that resembled a book.

"What's that?" Mary asked with a quizzical nod.

"It contains all my magic and gives me ideas," said the dog in the boot. Next came an iPad he claimed was named Luke. "Luke is a genius and does many things, he's taught me to pull animals out of these strings." He held up two strings, one orange and one blue, and they were tied with a knot.

Mary and John gasped when he pulled out a fox, then came a poodle with the word, Loves, followed by a cat wearing boxing gloves. One by one creatures appeared, and John and Mary were concerned by the skunk with a big tail. They were frightened he might attack, and how would they explain to Mother the smell on their backs?

The dog in the boot had to go! And Mary jumped up and told him so.

"I can't leave now, I'm just getting started! Don't be afraid, my animals are harmless."

Mary looked at the yard with the gigantic banner, and a flag, and all
those creatures running everywhere . . . which made her quite mad.
"I don't like your game, I don't like your show, now pack up your things,
you really must go!"

"I will, I will, don't get so upset, but first I must show you what I have left." He
pulled from his boot a huge watermelon made out of wood and an
Alexa made out of glass . . . which he placed on top of the watermelon in
their yard on the grass.

"This doesn't look good," said John with a start. "The sun is too hot and may
cause a spark." Then the dog in the boot began to bark. He barked low, he
barked loud, he barked to a song until Alexa sang along.

"Watch this, watch this," he said full of glee. "Alexa, show Mary and John what
you want them to see." She jumped on the watermelon made out of wood,
and lay there quietly as still as she could. Directly under the sun's beaming
rays, it wasn't long before she went up in a blaze.

The dog in the boot laughed and danced about while John and Mary looked
for something to put the fire out. The hose was too short, there was nothing
in sight, but the dog in the boot had one last surprise.

Out of his boot jumped an ice cube so big with two skinny legs and a mouth
with one lip. Before John and Mary could utter a word the ice cube showed
them he could sing like a bird.

"Howdy, howdy, I say to you and to you. Get out of my way, there is much
I must do!" He ran to Alexa and chatted away, "I'm here and I will melt the
fire away." He jumped on the fire so water could drop, put all of it out never
missing a spot.

Just then John and Mary heard Mother call out, "Come in and cool off
and rest for a spell."
They were nervous and scared and yelled at the dog, "Take your banner and
flag and creatures alike, flee while you can, Mother's almost in sight!"

Continued

"No need to be frightened," said the dog in the boot. "If you don't like my magic and tricks, I will leave you alone and my creatures and I will go home."

"What a mess, what a mess, what will we do? Mother's opening the door and I see her red shoe."

The dog in the boot snapped his fingers at last, then everything ran to his boot from the grass. When Mother arrived there was nothing in sight, and John and Mary never saw the dog in the boot take flight.

Mother smiled and put an arm around each one, "I guess you didn't hear me call because you were having so much fun."

John and Mary looked at each other and wondered if they should tell Mother.

THE END

Created by
Grandma
Debby Arthur Warner

With suggestions
From her amazing grandsons,
Leo and Allen Hildebran

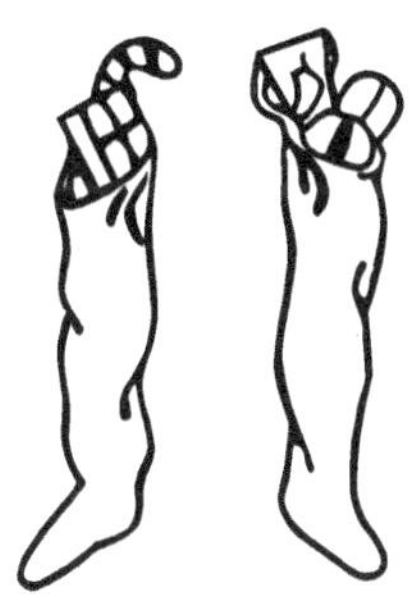

THE CHRISTMAS DREAM

Johnny woke from a wonderful dream and all he wanted that cold December morning was to close his eyes and fall back into dreamland. But the sun shining through the blinds prevented sleep from returning.

"Ugh, ugh, ugh!" he protested loudly. "I want my dream back!" Hearing mumbling coming from the bedroom, his mother came to see if he needed help.

"Johnny, what's wrong?" she asked, sitting down on the bed next to him. She could tell he was upset about something. The precocious six-year-old sat up, flung his legs over the side of the bed, and tearfully looked into his mother's eyes.

"Mom, I had the best Christmas dream anyone could ever have."

"Then why the tears?" she asked. "You look very sad for someone who just had such a wonderful dream."

Johnny hung his head. "Because it's the Christmas I wish we could have, but it was only a dream," he said mournfully. "Daddy lost his job because of the virus and you said Christmas would be different this year. We can't have presents or stockings or even baked ham like we did last year." He wiped his tears and once again looked at his mom. "Why can't we have a Christmas tree? There's lots of trees in the woods. If we have a Christmas tree, maybe Santa will come and leave us a gift." His mother pulled him close and rested her head on his.

"It's not that simple, Johnny. You have to get a permit before you can cut down a tree, and a permit costs money. We can't spend money on things we don't need when we need every penny for food and other necessities. It won't always be like this," she said, trying to console him. "Hopefully, next year will be different, and maybe it will be like the Christmas you dreamed about."

Johnny had an idea and jumped to his feet. "Well, I know what I'm going to do. I'm going to write a letter to Santa. If Santa knows Daddy lost his job and we can't have Christmas, maybe he can do something."

His mother looked a little concerned but tried to encourage him. "Okay, you write your letter to Santa, but remember that there are a lot of people in our situation, and Santa can't help everyone. He gets lots and lots of letters. He tries to do what he can, but he's a very busy man."

Johnny smiled. "I know, Mom, but he has lots of helpers and maybe one of them will read my letter to him."

"Maybe so," she said. She stood up and gave him a hug. "Let me know when you get your letter written, and I'll put a stamp on it and we'll take it to the post office." She smiled, kissed him on the forehead, and left him alone to think about his letter.

All that day, Johnny thought and thought about what he wanted to say to Santa. He knew he might need help from his mom on how to spell some of the words, but he had to be careful because he didn't want her to know what he was telling Santa. He wanted it to be a surprise. He didn't want her to know that he was asking Santa to make his dream come true.

That night as he drifted off to sleep, he slumbered once again into his Christmas dream. It was exactly the same as the night before. It started off with joyful singing voices outside his window. A fireman was carrying a large tree and entered his home. The singing got louder and more joyful. Women were carrying food and men had their arms full of Christmas ornaments and wrapped gifts. In his dream, after they were all gone, he ran downstairs in awe of what he saw. In the corner of the living room was a huge tree full of decorations and lights. On top of the tree was the biggest and brightest angel ornament he'd ever seen. Under the tree were so many gifts that there was hardly enough room for them—gifts for Mom and Dad and plenty for him. The kitchen counter was full of food, and when he looked in the refrigerator it was packed. Even the stockings on the fireplace mantle were so stuffed they couldn't have held one more thing. He danced and jumped around, and then one of the packages popped open and a puppy came out to greet him. He was so happy, and he wanted to stay in this dream forever.

When he woke up that morning, instead of being sad, he was excited and grabbed the letter to Santa that he'd been working on to add one more thing: "Santa, please leave a puppy if you have one." When he felt his letter was complete, he ran downstairs and asked his mom for an envelope. Now it was time to go mail it.

Johnny and his mother put their coats and gloves on, but when they opened the door, it was very cold and windy outside so they added a hat and scarf. On the way to the car, a huge gust of wind came up and blew Santa's letter right out of Johnny's hand.

"No! No!" he cried, running after it. The wind was very strong and blew the letter higher and higher until it was out of sight. Johnny's mother finally caught up to him, but she couldn't see the letter either. It had completely disappeared.

"Mom, where did it go? We have to find it or Santa will never know what I wrote. Come on," he urged, taking her hand and pulling her in the direction he wanted to go.

"Johnny, wait," she said. "We will never find the letter on foot. It's much too cold and the wind is brutal. Let's get the car and we'll drive around and see if it has fallen somewhere."

"Okay," he agreed, "but let's hurry!"

After driving around in circles for almost thirty minutes, it was clear that the letter was nowhere to be found, so Johnny and his mother went home.

"Johnny, you can write another letter and I'll take you to mail it tomorrow when the weather's better," she said in an effort to cheer him up.

"No, I can't," Johnny said sadly.

"Why not?"

"Because I already wrote everything I wanted to say and it took me a long time. My letter to Santa was exactly the way I wanted it to be and I know he would have read it. It was perfect. I could never write a letter like that again."

"Well, don't give up. It might make it to Santa. There's a good chance someone will find it and mail it for you."

He thought about what she said, then added, "Or maybe the wind blew it to the North Pole." Not having any idea how far away the North Pole was, he started gesturing with his hands so his mom would understand him. He explained that since it went so high and far, maybe it would find its way to Santa's door. And in his heart, he was going to hold on to that thought.

In the days leading up to Christmas something strange happened. Johnny's happy Christmas dream went away. Every night he hoped and longed for it, but it wouldn't come. On Christmas Eve he laid in bed, staring at the ceiling, and made one last wish. "If I can't have my Christmas this year, then could I please have the Christmas dream just one more time?" He repeated it over and over until he fell asleep.

Sometime in the early morning hours, he was wakened by joyful singing voices outside his bedroom window. At first, he thought he was asleep having his wonderful Christmas dream, but soon the singing voices got louder and more joyful, and he realized he was awake. He ran to the window just in time to see a fireman carrying a large tree into his house. Women were bringing food and men had their arms full of Christmas ornaments and wrapped gifts. He couldn't take his eyes off them. When there was nothing more to watch, Johnny ran downstairs and was in awe of what he saw. In the corner of the living room was a huge tree full of decorations and lights. On top of the tree was the biggest and brightest angel ornament he'd ever seen. Under the tree were so many gifts that there was hardly enough room to hold them—gifts for Mom and Dad and plenty for him. The kitchen counter was full of food, and when he looked in the refrigerator it was packed. Even the stockings on the fireplace mantle were stuffed and overflowing. Johnny was so excited he began to dance and jump around.

His parents were standing by the fireplace. "Mom, Dad—it's just like my dream!" he said with so much excitement. He was so happy that he forgot about the puppy in his dream. And just when he thought it couldn't get any better, a lid popped off one of the gifts and a very rambunctious black-and-white puppy scrambled out, running right into Johnny's arms.

"It really *is* my Christmas dream! It's the best Christmas ever!" He hugged his puppy and the puppy kept licking his face and wagging his tail. Johnny giggled and giggled. "I'm going to call you, Dreamer," he announced. Then he looked around the room trying to take it all in.

"Who were all those people?" he asked, looking at his mom. "Did Santa leave before I woke up?"

"Johnny, remember when I told you that Santa's a very busy man? Sometimes he uses many helpers and all those people wanted to help him. So you see, dear, your letter did get read," said his mom.

He looked around the room again and he couldn't stop smiling. His little heart was bursting with joy—not just for all the gifts and food that were brought, but he was also happy and thankful that so many people wanted to help Santa.

Holding his puppy, Johnny looked at his mom with a sparkle in his eye. "Mom, do you think when I grow up, I can help Santa?"

She gave him a big hug. "Johnny, I think Santa would like that."

Short Stories & Memoirs

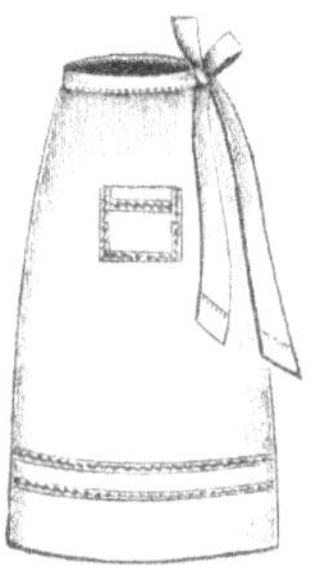

WHEN I WAS TWELVE

I'm twelve years old, sitting on a bus, and feeling very uncomfortable; yet, at the same time, very grown-up. I'm on my way to Lakewood from Freewood Acres. It's about a five-mile drive and I'm not sure that I want to go, but since I'm on summer break, my mother asked if I'd like to come to the café and work for a day. It seemed like a good idea at the time, but now I'm nervous. I'm a shy child and not sure of myself, especially around adults. My mother's a waitress at the café and friends with the owner, and I'm sure that's the reason I was allowed to come. I really don't know what I'll be able to do, probably just clean tables. Surely they wouldn't ask me to take an order—I'm only twelve.

The café is a small place down on Main Street and I've only been there once before. It was late afternoon when I was there and the lunch hour rush was over. I didn't get to see the madness of the chaotic lunch bunch in a hurry to eat so they could get back to work on time. I remembered it being slow, so I tell myself that this shouldn't be too difficult.

The bus stops at the end of Main Street. I get off and look for the Plymouth Café, which is about three blocks down the street on the right. Not being in a hurry, I take my time and window shop along the way, but when I approach the door to the Plymouth Café, I panic. It's lunch hour and it's packed! I nervously walk in and look for Mom. She's behind the counter—which is full—and she seems to be waiting on everyone at once. She immediately sees me and waves me over. As I walk by the tables, I notice that there isn't an empty chair anywhere, and I feel myself start to shake. I want to run out, get on the bus, go home, and hide in my bedroom.

Mom grabs my hand and pulls me behind the counter; she can see I'm visibly trembling. "Just watch me and do what I tell you—you'll be fine." Then she drops a bombshell; the other waitress scheduled to work didn't show up. She tells me she's glad I'm there because she can really use my help. I'm speechless and realize that my legs won't move. I watch my mother in disbelief . . . I didn't know she had ten hands!

The customers are yelling in their orders and she cheerfully responds to all of them as I remain frozen.

"Hey, Dixie, need more coffee over here."

"Okay, honey, I'll be right there."

"Dixie gal, where's my dessert?"

"Coming right up, sweetie."

Then the most amazing thing happens. My mother starts to sing, "You Are My Sunshine," and all ten of her hands are working at once.

"Debby, dear, would you bring some water over here to this table?" she says sweetly, pointing to the table in front of the window. Her infectious personality becomes as large as the bouffant hairdo framing her smiling face. She resumes singing, and now some of the customers are singing with her.

I look at the table. It's probably only fifteen feet from me, but my mind tells my legs that it's at least a mile away and my legs don't think they can walk that far.

"Debby, dear—the water!"

"Yes, Mom, I'm getting it." I finally get my legs to move and put ice in the water glasses. The ice is clanking against the glass as my hand shakes. I try to fill the glass with water and hope to silence the ice, but the water doesn't see the ice and pours on my hand and down my arm instead.

Mom rescues me, in one hand taking the tray of water to the table while her other nine hands continue to take care of everything else.

I ask to leave. She agrees, probably glad I'm going.

On the bus going home, I think about the lessons I've learned. Yes, believe it or not, I've learned much.

First . . . I will never be able to be a waitress.

Second . . . up until now, I thought of my mother as "just a waitress." But she isn't just a waitress; she's the best waitress!

And finally . . . it doesn't matter what you do in life, it just matters how you do it. If you approach everything enthusiastically—giving 100% of yourself—you will inspire someone else, regardless of how insignificant you may think your contributions are.

THE BED AND BREAKFAST

We climbed the stairway of the small old Victorian bed and breakfast and walked down the hall to our room. Halfway down, I jumped when I almost bumped into a pair of legs in overalls and boots dangling from the attic door in the ceiling—obviously the result of someone's warped sense of humor and a clear sign that our stay would be anything but uneventful.

Our little Maltese, Muffin, was with us and seemed nervous as she gingerly followed our lead. As we passed the room next to ours the door was wide open but it appeared to be void of guests. Our room was smaller, and had a door that opened to a little balcony, which I thought was nice. It also had a door on the side wall that we assumed connected to the room next to us.

Later that night as I was getting ready for bed it occurred to me that I never saw or heard anyone else checking in. I turned to my husband, Verl, and said, "I think we have the place to ourselves, which will be great because we won't have to share the bathroom." I grabbed my toiletry bag and headed towards the end of the hall. I expected Muffin to be right on my heels, but she stood in the doorway, shaking. She always followed me wherever I went, but I couldn't get her to budge. She was determined to stay where she was, so I proceeded to the bathroom on my own.

I had trouble falling asleep that night. I wasn't used to the sounds and creaks of an old building and, in the stillness, the noise was magnified. I started to doze off when I began to hear what sounded like scratching on the wall. I tried to ignore it, but it got louder and steadier. I shook Verl. "Listen," I whispered, "What's that noise?" Half asleep, he rolled over and waited.

"It could be a squirrel or a mouse in the attic. I'll get up and bang on the walls and scare it off," he said, as if that was going to make me feel better. Eventually, things did settle down and I was able to sleep until about four a.m. when I was aroused by a tapping sound. Still groggy, I wasn't sure where it was coming from. Verl stirred and immediately heard it, too. He checked the balcony door first, but then we realized it was coming from the door leading to the adjoining room. When we got closer, we could hear the doorknob turning. Verl grabbed the chair by the little desk and stuck it underneath the knob. All was quiet again but, for me, there was no returning to sleep.

Daylight was a welcome sight, and I looked forward to breakfast and having a chat with the owner, Barbara. I was anxious to know who might have been in the room next to ours and wondered if they would show up for breakfast. The quaint dining room was pleasant and full of color. The table was covered in an attractive deep-red cloth, and bright red floral napkins highlighted each of the six place settings. No one else had arrived yet so we had our choice of seats. Barbara, a petite mature woman, came bouncing in with a pot of coffee. Her long dull-blond static hair was pulled back, and her unmade face revealed deep crevices indicative of a hard life. I found it a contradiction to her energetic spirit.

"I'll start you with coffee," she said as she poured, "then I'll bring juice. Breakfast this morning will be a burrito, potatoes and fruit. It'll take me a little while, I don't have any help today. Hope you're not in a hurry." We assured her we weren't. She asked us where we were from then talked nonstop as if she'd known us for years. But before she left to check on our food, I was finally able to ask a question.

"Barbara, will anyone else be joining us?" I asked, assuming they must have come in late the night before since we didn't hear them arrive.

"There's no one else staying here except you two."

"But what about the people in the room next to us? We thought we heard someone in there." I didn't mention the tapping or the doorknob.

"The room's been empty all week, but you're not the first to hear sounds coming from that room when no one's been in there," she said with a smile as she went through the open doorway into the kitchen.

When she came back with our food, she proceeded to tell us about the time when another guest had complained that someone in the room snored all night and kept her awake. But again, the room was vacant. Jokingly, I asked if the place was haunted. She nodded. "Most of Cripple Creek is haunted. There are books on the coffee table in the parlor telling about some of the hauntings. But the snoring man might have just been a bum looking for a place to crash for the night," she said casually, as if that made for a better situation.

I was intrigued by Barbara, but it got even more interesting when I asked her to tell me a little bit about herself. She said that when she got married the first time, to her handsome Native-American husband, they were still in their teens. They lived on the reservation in a teepee. She paused, left the room, came back with a folder and handed it to me.

"This is a short story I wrote. It's about what happened to him. I always wanted to have it published, but never did. I'd like you to read it." She cleaned the table while I read.

I wasn't sure why she wanted me—a perfect stranger—to read it, but I was glad she did. It was a sad, beautifully written story of a young couple starting their life together on a reservation. It was a very different culture for Barbara, and one she was eager to be a part of. But a few weeks into their marriage, her young rambunctious mate went for a ride on his motorcycle and never returned. He wasn't wearing a helmet when he crashed and he died instantly.

I was still absorbing what this must have been like for Barbara at such a young age when she began to tell me about her second husband. They had been married for two years when he went hunting for a few days and didn't come back. She said he must have gotten lost during a snowstorm and froze to death. They didn't find his body until spring when the snow had melted. Just when I thought I'd heard it all, a man came into the B&B and went straight to the kitchen without saying a word. Barbara followed him. Verl and I were about to leave to go check on Muffin when Barbara returned.

"That's my ex-husband. I hated to call him, but I needed some work done and he knows the place." *Another husband?* I thought. She looked at us and shook her head, "I still can't stand him. He's the reason I have to take anger management classes."

I knew I shouldn't ask but I couldn't resist. "Why do you have to take anger management classes?"

"I caught him with another woman. That's why he's my ex. I was so mad that I twisted his balls until I almost ripped them off. He ended up in the hospital. They told me I could have killed him. They said I have anger issues. That's why I have to take the classes."

At that point I didn't know whether to be more concerned about the noises we heard or the woman running the bed and breakfast. Either way, I was fascinated and I knew I'd be back. Little did I know at the time that Barbara's bed and breakfast, and the experiences I had there, would be the inspiration for the setting of my first book, *Only by Chance in Cripple Creek*.

My Visits with Vivian
"The Night at the Hospital"

We were just finishing dinner when Lisa from the nursing home called. She said Vivian was complaining of chest pains and they were taking her to St. Mary's Hospital. It was the 4th of July and we had guests over for a cookout. Dessert had not yet been served. We excused ourselves to take the call, politely returned to the table, and calmly told of our situation. There was no panic, no urgency to leave—we had been through this before and it always ended well. Ten minutes later, our company respectfully declined dessert so we could be on our way.

At the hospital, we were told that my mother-in-law was down the hall in Cardiac A. When we walked into her room, I believe my husband and I simultaneously had the same reaction: How could someone of ninety-six years of age look even older? She was moaning in pain and wanting to tear off the blood pressure cuff that kept inflating and painfully tightening on her frail arm. She didn't understand that she needed to keep her arm still.

Verl stood at the foot of the bed and allowed me to be the one closest to Vivian. It was becoming more difficult for him to be around his mom—the more dependent she became, the more Verl wanted to distance himself. He felt helpless, inadequate, and at a loss. What could he do? How could he help? How could he fix her? How could he help her to be the independent, nurturing mother he'd always known? He couldn't and it hurt, so he retreated.

Her face lit up when she saw us, obviously pleased we were there and thankful not to be alone. We made small talk at first, then Verl and I told her about the fun we had on our recent trip to Hawaii, hoping it would divert her attention away from the pain. She smiled and said she remembered how much she enjoyed Hawaii when she visited, and then she got excited when I reminded her of just how much she loved to drink Chi Chis while she was there.

The nurse came in and brought a cup full of a clear blue liquid for Vivian to drink. He said it would taste like tea and she needed to drink all of it so they could take a picture of her stomach. The pains, it seemed, were not so much in her chest but in her stomach. After only one swallow, she said it didn't taste like tea and refused to drink it. The nurse left, leaving the task of getting it down her to me. I told Vivian to pretend that she was in Hawaii drinking a Chi Chi and every time she took a swallow to think of it as another Chi Chi going down. We were actually having fun and I had her giggling. Finally, she said she'd had enough and couldn't drink any more. I explained why she had to drink all of it, and once again pretended to serve a Chi Chi, but this time a sense of sadness went through me. As I zoomed in with the drink, I thought about the times I played airplane with my children in an attempt to get them to finish their meal. Now I was experiencing the same thing with a ninety-six-year-old instead of a three-year-old. Just when the final drop of the imaginary drink was finished, the nurse came back with another full cup of the so-called tea, and the process began all over again.

As we waited for them to come and take Vivian for X-rays, I tried hard to keep her attention away from her pain.

"Vivian, do you remember when you and I drove cross-country—just the two of us—two old gals all by themselves?"

"Oh, didn't we have fun!" she beamed. "I'll never forget that trip, that was so much fun!"

I watched the life come into her face as we talked about our road trip together. A few years back, when Verl decided to go hunting, I made plans to see my family in North Carolina and Georgia, then a visit to Tennessee. Verl's brother, Lowell, lived in South Carolina. I thought it would be a great time for Vivian to visit him, so I asked her if she'd like to drive cross-country with me. She was thrilled! We made arrangements to meet Lowell for lunch in Charlotte, North Carolina, and then Vivian would go to his home and spend time with his family as I continued on my journey to see mine. We made plans to meet up again on my way home so Vivian could come back with me.

I thought about the many conversations Vivian and I had all those days on the road and at night in the motels. She'd tell funny, interesting stories about her family, and we'd talk ourselves to sleep. At the time of that road trip, Verl and I had only been married for two years and Vivian was eighty-five—we didn't have years of knowing each other. I didn't see Vivian as a mother figure, and I didn't think of her in the same way that I would a friend or a sister. She was just a family member who I cared a lot about. But after that trip together, our relationship developed into a very unique friendship, and we had a tremendous amount of trust and respect for each other. She shared things with me that she wouldn't have shared with her four sons, things she felt that could only be understood by another woman. We were comfortable being ourselves with each other, knowing that if either of us did or said anything out of the ordinary, the other would understand.

I have wonderful memories of that road trip, and I couldn't have asked for a better traveling companion. I'm so glad I invited Vivian to go with me, but I'm even more grateful that she said yes.

My Visits with Vivian
"After the night at the Hospital"

Two days later, after our visit to the hospital, I went to see Vivian in the nursing home. In addition to wanting to know how she was feeling, I was anxious to talk to her about a memory she shared with Verl and me during her four-hour stay in the emergency room. After reminiscing about the cross-country trip that she and I had taken years before, she began telling us again about some of her other favorite memories. Although we'd heard these stories hundreds of times, we once again responded as though we were hearing them for the very first time. I thought it odd that in between moments of intense pain, mentally she seemed unusually sharp that evening. We nodded, smiled, and half listened to the familiar tales of earlier times. But soon she started talking about her grandmother and I found myself hanging on to every word in a way that I didn't remember doing before. Maybe that was because I'd only heard this particular story once or twice and I'd forgotten about it, or maybe it was because Vivian was ninety-six years old and I realized I may never hear these stories again. Whatever the reason, I was intrigued by Vivian's grandmother.

As the story goes, when Vivian was a little girl her grandmother was accidentally shot in the leg. According to Vivian, she said that when the men returned from hunting, they set their guns down—she didn't say where. Grandmother asked if the guns had been unloaded and was told they had. There was a four-year-old child in the room at the time, so Grandmother picked up the guns to move them out of the way when one fell to the floor and went off hitting her in the leg. She'd pushed the four-year-old out of the way just in time. The men put Grandmother on the kitchen table and amputated her leg, right then and there. No anesthesia, no sedatives—nothing! Actually, I had to ask about the anesthesia, because Vivian was more interested in telling us about the nub of a leg her grandmother was left with, and how as a child she used to love to play on it.

Before they took Vivian to X-ray, she added that Grandmother was a very positive woman, and she never let having only one leg get her down. She loved to travel and usually did so by train. With that, Vivian was wheeled down the hall, and I never had a chance to ask my burning questions.

Later that night as I lay in bed, I found myself thinking a lot about Vivian's grandmother. I thought about her strength, her character, and her positive attitude. I wondered if she ever knew how much joy she brought to her granddaughter by allowing her to bounce on the remains of the horrible tragedy she had endured. I wondered how she got around on one leg. I didn't think there could have been a prosthetic device at that time. Who were the men who returned from hunting? And who was the four-year-old child? I wanted to know more about Grandmother, and I was looking forward to my next visit with Vivian.

Friday, when I arrived at the nursing home, I found Vivian in the dining room. She was through eating and waiting to be wheeled out into the atrium. Her hair was combed nicely and she looked rather healthy, considering she'd spent most of the night on Wednesday in the emergency room.

She smiled when I greeted her. I wheeled her into the atrium and found a quiet spot so we could talk. I asked how she was feeling.

"Oh, fine," she said.

"Have you had any more pain since you came back from the hospital?"

She looked puzzled. "Hospital, when was I in the hospital?"

"The other night," I said.

"I don't remember being in the hospital. Why was I there?"

I explained and, to my surprise, she didn't remember anything about that night—not being there, not the pain, and no recollection of sharing stories with us. I brought up Grandmother. I could see some light begin to shine in her eyes, but it was dim. The sharpness wasn't there. Total recall wasn't present as it had been the other night. She acknowledged what information I fed her, but she didn't contribute any on her own. I was also surprised since Verl wasn't with me that she didn't ask about him.

On my way home I wondered how many other times she may not have been as clear-minded and I didn't notice because there wasn't a story I wanted to hear. And now I think about all those stories we've heard so often before, and I want to hear them again. But this time, I want to listen to them with my heart, and I can only hope I'll still have that opportunity.

My Visits with Vivian
"The Ring"

During one of my visits with Vivian, she looked at all the rings on my hand, and then looked at her bare fingers and sighed.

"I would like to have a ring," she said as she rubbed the area where her wedding rings had once been. "Your rings are beautiful. I used to have rings, but I don't anymore. I don't know why I stopped wearing them."

She didn't ask about her wedding rings. It seemed she'd forgotten that she had given them to Verl and me for safekeeping. We encouraged her to do so after she kept misplacing them. She'd forget where they were and then worry that she might've lost them. We told her we could put her rings in our safety deposit box for safekeeping and anytime she wanted to wear them, we'd bring them to her. She liked that idea. The first year she asked about them all the time, but this past year she hadn't mentioned them.

I quietly watched as she continued to play with her finger and pretend she was turning a ring. "Vivian, I have some extra rings. I'll bring you one," I said.

"Would you really?" she asked, eyes glowing.

I smiled and assured her I'd bring one the next time I came. I knew she might not remember the conversation, but I was pleased that—at least for the moment—she had something to look forward to. I'd sold fashion jewelry in the past, so I had a few samples on hand.

Wednesday, after my morning writing class and lunch with a friend, I took my selection of rings and went to the nursing home to visit Vivian. It was late summer and the day was too beautiful to be indoors. I wheeled Vivian outside so she could enjoy the fresh air. Even though the temperature was hovering around ninety degrees, she was heavily clothed.

She stared at the canvas bag hanging from my arm. I sat down on the bench in front of her and took out a box containing twelve different styles of rings and showed it to her.

"Which one do you like?" I asked. She beamed and pointed to a large antique silver one with a very simple design. "Try it on," I suggested before realizing that I had no idea the size of any of the rings. A few of them—all costume—had been given to me by my cousin when my aunt passed away. *Oh my,* I thought, *what if none of them fit!* She took it out of the box and put it on her ring finger, and I'll be darned—it fit!

"I like it!" she said with a smile.

"Try on another," I encouraged. She removed the first choice and picked up a dinner ring with red and clear stones. To my surprise, it also fit.

"Isn't this beautiful?" she exclaimed, admiring it with great delight. Then she took it off and neatly placed it in the box with the rest of the rings.

"Would you like to try on another?" I asked.

"No, I don't think so, but they're all beautiful."

I continued to hold the box in front of her. "Look at all of them and choose the one you like the best."

She studied each one carefully. "Am I supposed to take one?"

"Yes. You may have any one you'd like."

"Oh, boy, let's see . . . I think I like this one." She took the large antique silver one she had tried on first. Once it was placed on her finger, she twirled it a few seconds, then looked at me. I wondered why she'd chosen that particular ring, but before I could ask, she moved on to something else.

"You know, I've had a good life."

"Yes, you have," I said, putting the rest of the rings away and making myself comfortable. I could see in her eyes she had a story to tell.

"There were seven of us kids," she began. "We always lived in a large house. My father liked a large house. He built my mother a big two-story home. That was a great house! It had a stairway going up from the front as you came in the door, and also one when you came in the back door. My brothers and I used to run the long hallways upstairs, and then run down one set of stairs and up the other. Round and round we'd go." She was gesturing with her hands, showing me how they would do it.

"My twin sisters, Jean and June, would sometimes come home from school and tell my parents they had friends coming over later. My dad knew what that meant. We had two adjoining rooms with a large dividing door that could be pushed back into the wall. Dad would push the doors back, making one big room out of the two, and roll up the carpet so the girls could dance. I loved to watch them, but I never joined in. I didn't like to dance, but oh did we have fun as kids." She was still smiling as she relived her youth when another thought came to her. "And we had a live-in maid. She had her own room. She'd go home on weekends and come back on Mondays."

I listened to Vivian and thought about *my* childhood. It certainly paled in comparison. I tried to think of an occasion when I felt as joyful within my own family, but none came to mind.

"Your father worked in a stone quarry, didn't he?" I asked, trying to imagine the expense of a live-in maid, seven children, and a large house. I'm sure a dollar went a lot further back in his day . . . but still.

"Oh, yes, he was a granite cutter and the foreman. Later my brother Louis worked with him. They made headstones for graves. You know, my younger brother, Elton, died when he was only twenty-four. He had a heart attack. Dad and Louis made his headstone—imagine that."

I thought about how difficult that had to be. "Vivian, I can imagine it was a very sad time for all of you."

"I've often thought about how hard it must have been for my dad and Louis to make Elton's tombstone."

"I'm sure it must have been painful," I said, "but I do think it's special that they were able to do that for Elton." She nodded, and then her thoughts seemed to drift off. I could tell she was getting tired.

"I'm trying to think of when I heard from Louis last. It's been a while. I bet it's been at least a couple of years," she said.

I didn't say anything, because I wasn't sure what to say. Louis died twelve years ago. I just listened, not knowing what time frame she was in. When I left, I wondered if there would come a time when she wouldn't remember me.

NOT AN ORDINARY ROSE

On Friday at noon, Gloria once again comes to the park to eat her lunch and study the unobserving stranger with the red rose. This time she's coaxed her co-worker and friend, Joan, into coming with her. The air seems especially fresh today with the beginning scents of budding flowers and blossoming spring trees.

They sit on the bench closest to the dogwood tree for two reasons: it's Gloria's favorite spot and it also gives her the best vantage point to study her subject—the stranger with the red rose.

Joan takes her lunch out of the bag when Gloria whispers, "Look, there he is!"

Joan looks around. "Where?"

"Over there," says Gloria, pointing ahead.

Following Gloria's finger as it curves to the left toward the pond, Joan notices a handsome, distinguished-looking gentleman with premature graying hair, sitting on the bench closest to the pond, holding a single long-stemmed red rose. "Why do you suppose he's here?" she asks.

"I don't know. The last two months since I've been coming, he's here every Friday, and he always has one red rose. I was fascinated the first couple of weeks, but now my curiosity has the better of me. I never see anyone join him, nor do I see him leave. Of course, I'm only here during my lunch hour on Friday. Mrs. Tilley is my last appointment before lunch, and she can be very ornery and demanding at times, and that can mean it takes me longer to do her hair."

"I don't know how you put up with that woman," remarks Joan.

"Believe me, I wouldn't if she wasn't a friend of my mother's."

As they continue to eat, eyes focused on the stranger, it appears to Joan that the gentleman seems sad. "I wonder if he comes here to mourn the death of a loved one," she says as she swallows her last bite.

"I have no idea. Sometimes he looks sad or deep in thought, and other times he's looking around as though he's waiting for someone. I've decided I want to know more about him. Next week I think I'll sit next to him and see what happens."

"That doesn't sound too wise," says Joan.

"Maybe not, but I'm going to do it anyway." They both glance at their watches and realize it's time to get back to the shop. Gloria is already anticipating next Friday.

The week drags on as Gloria anxiously waits for Friday to arrive. Wouldn't you know, Mrs. Tilley is not only fifteen minutes late but she's also in one of her moods. Pudgy Mrs. Tilley gripes again about the chair being too small as Gloria murmurs under her breath, "Doesn't she realize if she'd lose weight the chair wouldn't be too small?" And, of course, today she wants her hair shampooed twice and the five-minute conditioner added. Finally, thirty minutes behind her usual time, Gloria leaves for the park.

She's in luck; the stranger is still there and again all alone. She slowly walks over to where he is and tries to be discreet as she quietly sits next to him. He's staring down at the rose he holds in his hands resting between his knees, lost in thought, unaware that someone has invaded his privacy.

"Excuse me," she says thoughtfully, "I hope I'm not intruding."

The stranger looks up, for the first time aware of Gloria's presence. "Not at all," he replies, looking back at the rose he twirls between his fingers.

After several minutes of uncomfortable silence, Gloria ventures, "The rose, it's . . . it's very pretty."

"Yes, it is, isn't it? But then, aren't they all?" he asks and turns to face her. She's surprised by the warmth and depth his soft blue eyes seem to convey.

"No . . . I mean, yes . . . well, actually I prefer yellow roses," she replies, "although the rose you're holding is very beautiful."

"Interesting. I always thought red was the color of choice for most women."

"I guess it is, but to me it's depressing. Maybe that's because I've only gotten them during sad events in my life. Yellow, on the other hand, seems to have a cheerful and uplifting energy that I enjoy being around. Not that I've received many yellow roses, but if I were to receive roses, I'd like them to be yellow."

The gentleman does not respond but continues to stare at the rose.

"Oh, listen to me, I do have a tendency to ramble on. I'm truly sorry if I've said anything to offend you," she says, realizing that referring to the red rose as depressing was probably not the best thing she could have done.

He smiles. "No, actually I was thinking it's rather nice to have someone to talk with. I've been coming here for four months and this is the first time I even noticed anyone else being here. Surprisingly, this place is very quiet on Fridays during lunch hour. Well, to be honest, I've been preoccupied, so I haven't really paid attention if anyone might be here."

"Yes, you have been deep in thought." Before she can finish, the gentleman looks at her with a puzzled look. "Oh, here I go again. Okay, I confess I have noticed you sitting over here every Friday holding one red rose and, yes, I've wondered why. Don't worry, since I have to get back to work, you're saved from having to come up with an awkward excuse as to why you don't want to respond."

Gloria—feeling really embarrassed—gets up to leave. As she's walking away, she hears him say, "Young lady, I seem to be at a disadvantage. You've been watching me for weeks, and I don't even know your name."

She turns to face him, continuing to walk backwards as she shouts, "Gloria, Gloria Gardner. And you are?"

"Paul Richardson," he yells as she begins to disappear.

For the next several weeks, Paul and Gloria share the park bench and become comfortable exchanging little details about themselves. Paul still brings the red rose and begins to explain its significance.

"Gloria, five months ago I was to be married. The day of our wedding my fiancé started having second thoughts. I took her to the park to talk, hoping to ease her concerns. She decided she was too confused as to what she really wanted and needed more time. It was on a Friday at noon; she was holding a red rose pulled from one of our wedding bouquets. Realizing I couldn't talk her out of her fears, I promised to wait—for a while. I told her that every Friday, I would wait in the park with one red rose. If we were to have a life together, she would come and take the rose. If she hadn't come by the end of six months— which will be three weeks from now—I would no longer wait."

"Thank you, Paul, for sharing that with me," replies Gloria feeling closer to this person who she hardly knows. Now with only three weeks left, Gloria is hoping Paul will come to the park without the red rose, hoping he'll realize he doesn't need this undeserving woman.

During the next couple of weeks Gloria is uneasy, feeling nervous and not understanding why. She tells herself it's out of concern for Paul; after all, they have developed a unique friendship these last few weeks.

It's June 15th, D-Day. Gloria wakes up with a headache, feeling very tense and wondering if she should not go to the park. What if "she" comes? What if "she" doesn't come, what then? Reluctantly, she gets ready for work and then remembers that Mrs. Tilley is to get a perm today.

The jitters won't stop, and for every perm rod she puts in Mrs. Tilley's hair, another pops out.

"Gloria, you seem to be having a problem with my hair today," observes Mrs. Tilley. "Are you using different rods?"

"No, Mrs. Tilley, same rods. Your hair seems a little more stubborn than usual."

"Well, if you ask me," says Mrs. Tilley in her annoying, whiny voice, "I think you have other things on your mind that you think are more important than fixing my hair. When your mother fixed my hair, she was always very conscientious."

Gloria ignores the remarks, takes a deep breath, and tries to calm down. She finishes with Mrs. Tilley and, even though a little late, she walks slowly to the park. By now Paul knows her routine—sometimes she runs behind. Paul will be there, she thinks, unless . . .

As she approaches the park, she stops. No one is on the bench by the pond, so "she" must have come and taken the red rose, thinks Gloria. She can't make herself go over by the pond, so she sits on her old favorite bench by the dogwood tree and watches. No one comes so she leaves, confused by the emotions she's feeling.

The week is slow and painful, but once again on Friday, Gloria decides to go to the park one last time—if for no other reason than to try and sort out her feelings.

The bench is empty. She wanders over, sits down and stretches her arm out to the vacant space next to her. Feeling something, she looks down to see a long-stemmed rose. It takes her a moment to realize that *this* is no ordinary rose. This rose is yellow. Before she has time to guess where it came from, she hears a voice.

"I didn't come to the park last week."

Looking up, she sees Paul. "Why?" she asks.

"Sometimes we think we know what we want. Then, for whatever reason, our circumstances change, and what we thought we wanted doesn't seem so important anymore." Extending his hand toward hers, he asks, "Would you join me for a cup of coffee? I think it's time we got to know each other . . . away from the park."

Smiling, clutching the yellow rose, Gloria reaches up to take Paul's hand.

THE PALACE

The house on the hill had been empty for years. The paint was chipping and the lawn had gone to weeds, but to me there was an eerie charm about it. The old oak trees looked peaceful as they slept through winter but, in full bloom during summer, they looked protective of the dying house.

I'm not sure when I first became intrigued with the place or during which season I enjoyed observing it the most. I guess you could say I was drawn to it as if by a magnet, so much so that I began to walk by it on a regular basis, hoping someone would eventually move in and give it life. In an odd way, after many months of strolling by and studying the deserted estate, I felt as though we had developed a unique relationship. I began a ritual of visiting every day throughout the year with the exception of October 31—Halloween. Something about that day gave me pause, and I felt the need to avoid it.

I'd heard the stories of the trick-or-treaters who braved the spooky night and walked the premises of the vacant house. A few of them even ventured up to the front door. I'd heard the tales of the weird sounds coming from the house. Children tripped as they ran away. Most were older children who weren't accompanied by a parent. And then three teenagers claimed that a mysterious wind came out of nowhere and forcefully ripped the bags of candy from their hands, sending the contents flying everywhere. The wind howled as they ran for their lives, but when they got to the road—just a few hundred yards away—all was calm again. How much was factual depended on whom you talked to. But even if I had assumed it was nothing more than the imagination of frightened kids on a spooky night, I still stayed home on October 31.

Once again, as Halloween approached, I thought about how beautiful fall had been. Spectacular golden and bright yellows illuminated the weeping willow trees while soft and vivid hues of reds and oranges dazzled the oaks and maples. I usually took a walk before dinner but on October 30 and Mischief Night—the night before Halloween when the mischievous ventured out and threw eggs at cars and houses and adorned the trees with toilet paper—I decided to eat early and then take my walk. The local weatherman had promised a colorful sunset, and I wanted to make sure that I didn't miss it. I went a different route so I could get the full view of the sun going down and I wasn't disappointed, but I came back by way of the "palace"—a nickname I had affectionately given the old rundown estate.

The night air was crisp but mild for late October. When I got to the palace I paused, as I had many times before, but this time something felt different. I lingered, staring up at the windows on the second floor. Everything was so still and quiet that I didn't even hear a car passing by. Before I knew it, I was walking through the yard towards the front door. It seemed silly, especially since I knew no one was there, but I knocked on the weather-beaten door. To my surprise, it creaked open about four inches. I stood stunned, wondering whether I should go in or run in the opposite direction. My legs wobbled and I didn't think I could move either way. After what seemed like an eternity, a slight breeze blew and the door opened wider.

Soon my paralysis lifted and I didn't realize that I had stepped inside. It was dark, so very dark. At first, I couldn't see anything, but my eyes quickly adjusted and I could see a faint flickering light at the end of a long hallway. I wondered if it was a candle, but if it was, then that meant someone was here, or at least had been.

Curiosity replaced my fear and I forged onward. Could this old rundown estate that I had admired for years actually be inviting me in? I followed the dim light, but it was difficult to see and I kept bumping into things. The floor creaked with each step and the large room felt cold and damp, but when I got to the hallway, I felt a warm welcoming breeze. Then I heard the front door slam shut. I moved slowly, not wanting to disturb anything or anyone.

The light began to fade. I became anxious, and I knew I had to get to the light before it went out. I could hear unidentifiable sounds and echoes coming from rooms that I passed—just rumblings from an old deserted house, I told myself, but then it was pitch black. The light was gone. I couldn't even see my hand in front of me. Shaking, I stood there, and then I felt something or someone take my hand and pull me forward. I didn't know where I was going, but there was no time to think—I just went. I felt a presence behind me but I didn't dare turn around; I doubt that I could've seen anything anyway. My mind was blank. I was numb and, at that particular moment, void of any form of emotion. I just knew that I had to do what I was silently told.

Gently, I was led into a very large room. By the soft light coming from the distant corner, I could see it was a large room. Once inside, I saw someone adjusting the kerosene lantern. It was then that I recognized the person who'd been guiding me. It was Martha Jeffries! She went on a hiking trip years ago but was never seen again. They searched for months but gave up when winter came. She was the owner of the palace.

Two men and another woman came closer to me and I realized that I knew them, too. They all looked frail but otherwise OK for having been missing for years and presumed dead.

Robert Collins, the tall gangly man, was the president of our local bank. He went fishing in the ocean one day and never returned. His boat was found but not his body. The shorter man with the balding head was Mr. Peters, owner of the flower shop on Main and Broadway. His nephew ran it now. Mr. Peters left for a cross-country trip to spend the summer with his sickly brother, but he never made it to his brother's house. His abandoned car was found at a rest area 500 miles from home. It was assumed he met with foul play. Then there was the popular psychologist, Sandra Atkins. Many of the townspeople had visited her for one reason or another because she was so easy to talk to. Everyone was devastated when she didn't show up for work one day, and she was never seen again. The leads went cold and eventually they quit looking for her. Why were they all in Martha's deserted house? Why didn't they let anyone know that they were alive? I was soon to find out.

Martha, looked much older now, hair long and gray. I noticed that her posture wasn't as exact as it used to be as she walked me over to an old Victorian chair and asked that I take a seat. Robert, Mr. Peters, and Sandra joined her on the rundown sofa in front of me. Martha spoke first.

"Please don't be afraid. We need help. We've been watching you come by this place for years, hoping an opportunity would bring you inside." I was so dumbfounded I couldn't find my words. Sandra leaned over and took my hand.

"We have to trust you because you're our last hope. Do you understand?"

"I'm not sure. I'm confused. If you're not dead, then why are you here?"

"For our protection," Robert said. "Someone wants us dead, so we had to pretend to be dead. We've been living—if you can call it that—for the last decade in the shadows."

"Who wants you dead? And why? How have you been able to live? Where do you get food and water to sustain you? Does anyone know you're alive?" Once I found my voice, the questions kept coming.

"John will explain more," Martha said. Short, balding, kind Mr. Peters leaned forward. I didn't know his first name was John. I'd only known him as Mr. Peters—the nice helpful gardener who loved his floral shop.

"If I remember correctly," he said, "I believe your name is Stacy. You used to come in the shop every few weeks and pick out a floral arrangement for your dining room table. You said it made you feel good to have fresh flowers in the house, even if no one was coming. I hope you've kept up the tradition."

I smiled, pleased that he remembered me. "I'm sorry to say, I haven't kept the tradition. The week after you disappeared, Dr. Atkins went missing." I looked at Sandra. I had been to see her a few times because I was having trouble sleeping. I found her to be warm and comforting. I liked her very much. I focused my attention back on Mr. Peters. "The four of you went missing about a week apart from each other. It was all too surreal. Mr. Peters, I guess you're the one who's going to explain to me what's going on."

"Please listen carefully," he began. "We're the lucky ones we disappeared before we could be murdered. My cousin, Father Daniels, is the only one who knows we're alive. He's the reason the rest of us joined Martha here. She confided in him, and he knew eventually she would try to sneak back into the house when it was safe to do so. In the meantime, he hid her in the Parish House as he did Robert, Sandra, and me."

I was beginning to wonder if I'd ever find out what caused all of them to secretly take refuge in the old estate.

Mr. Peters continued, "Stacy, are you familiar with Sheriff Tom Meeker?"

"I've never met him, but I know of him. I've seen him on the news and I've heard stories about him. I understand he's very powerful and mean."

"Yes, he is. He wants to control the town and every business in it, but the more he controls, the worse he becomes."

Martha spoke up. "Sheriff Meeker is an overzealous, controlling narcissist who resents anyone's success unless he can benefit from it. The man is deranged! He thinks he's entitled to be compensated since he protects the community. I own this estate and the property surrounding it but it doesn't produce an income, so I never had a problem with the sheriff until he learned that I owned the buildings on Main Street between First and Second, that's when he paid me a visit. He wanted a percentage of the monthly rent I received from my tenants. He said if I refused, my tenants and their businesses wouldn't be protected, and he couldn't be responsible for what might happen. He was a bully and very intimidating, and I was afraid not to go along with him. Only when he wanted to increase the percentage did I stand up to him and refuse to give him any more. A few days later one of my tenants mysteriously vanished, and I realized I was in a dangerous situation."

I was trying to digest everything that was being said, but I couldn't understand how one person was able to do this to so many people and not get caught. I posed the question. Robert answered.

"By intimidation and threatening to spread lies about their personal lives and business practices, eventually causing them to go out of business. No one really talked to each other about it. I think each person thought they were the only one that this was happening to. Maybe since I was president of the bank, Sheriff Meeker decided not to try and extort money from me, but he did get to me in another way. At the time, I was totally unaware of what he was like until the day when I was in old man Simpson's barber shop getting a haircut, and he walked in. Stacy, do you remember Gus Simpson?"

I had to think for a minute. I'd never met Mr. Simpson, but I knew he was friendly and had a good business. I used to walk by his place on my way to Mr. Peters's floral shop. He was only a couple of doors down, and he'd wave to me as I went by. That's all I knew of him.

"I heard he had a heart attack several years ago," I said. "Wasn't that the same year you all disappeared?"

"Yes, it was," said Robert. "I was in the barber chair and Gus was cutting my hair when the sheriff came in. It was a slow Monday morning and I was the only customer. The sheriff walked over to Gus and pushed him away from the chair. He started yelling at him and said, 'You were supposed to call me by the end of the day on Friday and I don't like being ignored!' The sheriff towered over the little old man, but Gus didn't appear to be afraid. He looked up at the sheriff and said he worked hard for his money, his customers trusted him, and he wouldn't let a crooked sheriff steal from him. I didn't understand what was going on, and both of them seemed to forget that I was there. Gus's response infuriated the sheriff and he grabbed him by the neck, pushed him up against the wall, and reminded him that he was the sheriff in town. Gus better comply if he knew what was good for him. Then he threw the poor old man to the floor and Gus started gagging and grabbed at his heart. Sheriff Meeker coldly stepped over him. Realizing that I was still in the chair and witnessed what just took place, he pointed his finger at me and said, 'You never saw me here, and if you know what's good for you, you'll keep your mouth shut.' He looked back at Gus, who was struggling to breathe, then said, 'You'd better call 911 for your friend. And remember, I was never here.' With that, he pushed the door open and stomped out. By the time the paramedics got there, Gus Simpson was already deceased. He died of a heart attack."

I was horrified! How could anyone be so cruel to a sweet old man? I knew this was just the tip of the iceberg, and I was sure there was plenty more to come. Robert went on to tell me that the sheriff showed up at his bank the next day and warned him again to keep his mouth shut.

"Robert, at what point did you decide to fake your own death?"

"When Sheriff Meeker became paranoid every time he saw me talking to someone. He began to come around on a daily basis. The final straw was when he told me to watch my back because I could end up like Mr. Simpson. I knew what he meant, and I knew I had to do something before that happened."

I took a deep breath, almost afraid to hear anymore. I looked at Mr. Peters and Sandra. "I guess each of you had a similar situation." They nodded, but I was more curious about the popular therapist since she was a medical professional, and her office was in the medical complex. As I was still wondering about this, Sandra began to explain.

"When I saw that Tom Meeker had made an appointment, I assumed he was coming in as a client. It didn't take me long to realize his true motive. We no sooner had our hellos out of the way, when he got straight to the point. To help keep my practice safe, he wanted ten percent of all fees I collected. I refused. He then indicated that my reputation might suffer if my clients discovered I was sharing their personal and confidential information with other clients. I reminded him that not only did my clients have the utmost trust in me, but I was highly respected by my colleagues. They would quickly put an end to the rumors and work to find out where they came from. He huffed out of my office and I naïvely thought that was the end of it. I didn't know the sheriff was doing this to most of the businesses in town until Bill Owens became my client. You may not know him, but he owned the gas station on the outskirts of town. He was giving the sheriff ten percent off the top of his gross income, but then the sheriff decided he wanted fifteen percent, and that's when Bill came to see me. He was barely making a living as it was, but he was too scared to refuse. He was so stressed, he could hardly eat or sleep. He thought he was safe confiding in me, but when the sheriff found out that Bill was a client of mine, his body was found in a ditch behind the station. I knew it was only a matter of time before I was next."

My head was spinning. This was too much for anyone to understand. I was beginning to feel like I was in a nightmare. How could this be real? How could this happen? And how was I supposed to help? I wanted to be back out-side. I wanted to be on my evening walk. I didn't want to know any of this.

Martha put her hand on my shoulder. "Stacy, we need you to help us. Please!" she said.

"But what can I do?"

"We have a plan," she continued. "We've been planning this for a very long time. This evil man has to be stopped."

"But how?" I asked.

"We'll take care of everything," said Mr. Peters. "All you have to do is come by here tomorrow night, then call the sheriff and tell him you think someone has broken into Martha Jeffries's house."

"Tomorrow night is Halloween," I protested. "I don't go out on Halloween. I'll come the night after."

"It has to be tomorrow night," said Robert. "There will be a lot going on with the trick-or-treaters, and the sheriff will be more inclined to believe the estate was broken into on Halloween night than the night after."

"Please," said Sandra, "We need you and you won't have to do much. When the sheriff arrives, tell him that you thought two teenagers in Halloween costumes entered the back door, but since it was dark, you weren't sure. You walked up to the house and heard voices and that's when you decided to call him. Stacy, make sure you don't go inside the house. When the sheriff enters, you leave immediately, and we'll take care of the rest."

"What do you mean by, *the rest*?" I questioned.

"That's not for you to worry about," said Robert. "Everything will work out the way it should, and no harm will come to you. I promise."

I believed Robert's promise. And even though I didn't know what was going to happen, I knew I had to help. We said goodbye and I assured them I'd be back promptly at seven o'clock on Halloween night, and I was.

I walked around to the back of the palace as I was instructed so I wouldn't be seen at the front door by trick-or-treaters. As I was approaching, I realized that no one knew where I was. All kinds of thoughts were running through my head and I hoped whatever they had planned didn't backfire, because I didn't want to be the sheriff's next victim.

I began walking up the steps when Robert opened the door and ushered me in. He pointed to a room on my right, which I could hardly make out in the darkness.

"After you call the sheriff and explain that you saw two teenage boys go into the house," he said, "tell him you'll wait for him on the back steps because that's where they entered. When the sheriff gets here and is fully inside the house," Robert pointed to the room he just showed me, "tell him that you heard loud noises coming from in there, and then you leave immediately and go home."

I do believe that if I fully understood what was happening, I don't think I would have asked my next question. "But Robert, if I leave, won't the sheriff become suspicious?"

He smiled at me. "Stacy, there's no need to worry about the sheriff. Everything will be fine." Before I could say another word, Martha walked up to me and rubbed my arm.

"You look very tired, dear. Please do what Robert asks of you, and then go home and rest. Maybe we'll see you tomorrow," she said, giving me a warm reassuring smile.

I did what I was asked to do. I called the sheriff and assured him I'd wait until he arrived. Once he was inside the house, I pointed through the darkness in the direction where I said I heard the noises, and then I left. It all felt odd, but it *was* Halloween after all, and I don't like going out on Halloween night.

On my walk home, I couldn't help but wonder what might be going on at the palace. I couldn't imagine that Robert, Martha, Sandra, or Mr. Peters were capable of doing anything bad—they were all too nice. I started thinking about what they might have in mind. Maybe they're going to confront Sheriff Meeker and secretly record him so they'd have the evidence they need to take to the FBI. *Yes, that's what they must be doing,* I assured myself.

After a restless night, I was feeling very anxious. I knew I had to go to the palace and make sure everyone was okay. When I arrived, I was surprised to see Sheriff Meeker's car still in the driveway. I felt concern for my new friends, and I also felt concern for myself. What if I knock on the door and the sheriff won't let me leave? But I didn't hesitate for long: I knew I had to go inside.

I tried to open the front door first, but it was locked and no one came when I knocked. I went around to the back door and it was also locked. Again, I knocked, but nothing happened. I put my ear against the door hoping to hear something, but everything was quiet. Vigorously I pounded with my fist, but it was all in vain. I wasn't sure what to do next. If they were secretly recording the sheriff and he caught them, then they certainly would be in danger. I had to do something but I couldn't think straight. I remembered Mr. Peters saying that his cousin, Father Daniels, had helped them once before. I decided to pay him a visit.

I was relieved that Father Daniels was the first person I encountered, because as soon as I opened my mouth to speak, I couldn't stop babbling. I'm sure he thought I was some crazy deranged person, but when I mentioned Mr. Peter's name, he whispered for me to follow him and led me to his office. Once inside, he closed the door and gestured for me to sit down.

"Please," he said, "start from the beginning and slowly tell me what's going on." I took a deep breath and calmly tried to explain what had transpired over the last couple of days. Father Daniels sat quietly for a moment, as if weighing my words. I was beginning to wonder if he believed anything I said. After all, it was pretty unbelievable, but he already knew they were in hiding.

After what seemed like an eternity, he finally spoke. "I'll look into this and find out what's going on. In the meantime, I want you to stay here where you'll be safe. Sister Adeline can be trusted, and I'll ask her to stay with you until you hear further from me. Please let her know if you want anything to eat or drink. She will see to your needs." I assured him I'd be okay, but I was anxious to find out what was happening.

After a few hours I began to feel nervous, and then the door opened and in walked Father Daniels, Mr. Peters, Robert, Martha, and Sandra. I was excited and relieved! They were alive and okay! They each came over and gave me a hug.

"Stacy, if it wasn't for your help, I don't think we'd be here," said Mr. Peters.

I was confused and I still wasn't sure exactly how I might have helped. I looked at Martha and said, "I saw Sheriff Meeker's car at your home this morning. How did you get away from him, and do you know why he's still there?"

Compassionate, Father Daniels took my hand and proceeded to tell me the most outrageous story I think I've ever heard. Robert, Mr. Peters, Martha, and Sandra sat quietly, nodding occasionally in agreement. Here's what I was told:

Evidently, once the sheriff entered the old house he went into a room, that—due to rain damage—had a large hole in the floor. Martha had stayed away from the room because the leak in the roof had worsened over the years causing the floor to rot away. And since she was in hiding, she couldn't have it repaired. After the sheriff went into the damaged room, Martha and the others left and went to the rectory to hide in the basement. They took a shortcut through Martha's backyard and into the woods. It was still a mile from the palace, but they made it without incident. When Father Daniels and I spoke earlier, he obviously had no idea that they were there. After he left me, he went to Martha's and when he couldn't get an answer, he called the police and told them that the sheriff's car had been seen there overnight but there was no sign of him.

I wanted to ask if anyone warned the sheriff about the dangerous conditions inside the room, but then it occurred to me that it was the same room I pointed out to the sheriff, telling him it's where I heard the noises. I had all kinds of thoughts and questions going through my head, but I couldn't get myself to utter a word. I felt numb, just like I did the first time I entered the palace. It was all too surreal. Nothing much registered after that.

I'm not sure when I left the rectory, I was in a daze and I barely remember unlocking my front door. The last thing I recalled hearing—before everyone smiled and said their goodbyes—was for me to try to forget that I was ever at Martha's house. And that no matter what, in my heart I should always know that I did a good thing.

The next day, as I was sitting on my sofa trying to make sense of everything, I glanced at the TV and I couldn't believe what I saw. Streaming across the bottom . . . breaking news . . . Sheriff Meeker found dead in an abandoned house. It appeared that he fell through a hole in a rotting floor and hit his head on the basement concrete.

During the next few days, the officer who found the sheriff's body said that, after talking with some of the businessowners in town, he was learning more about the sheriff and what a corrupt person he really was. He added that he thought the sheriff might have gone into the abandoned estate with the intention of taking anything he could find of value. After all, it was Halloween night, and who would have questioned him?

"Everyone can rest easier now," said the officer. "The sheriff is no longer a threat. His evil deeds caught up with him." He looked over to his right, "I'd like to take time now to introduce you to four outstanding citizens who purposely disappeared for years because of being intimidated and threatened by the sheriff. Hopefully they can now live a normal and fear-free life," he said. The cameraman zoomed in on Robert, Mr. Peters, Sandra, and Martha. I watched as people crossed the street, clapping and cheering as they waited for the newscast to end so they could greet them.

Should I have gone to the authorities and told them what I knew? Maybe. But before you pass judgment, ask yourself this question: If you were in my situation, what would you do?

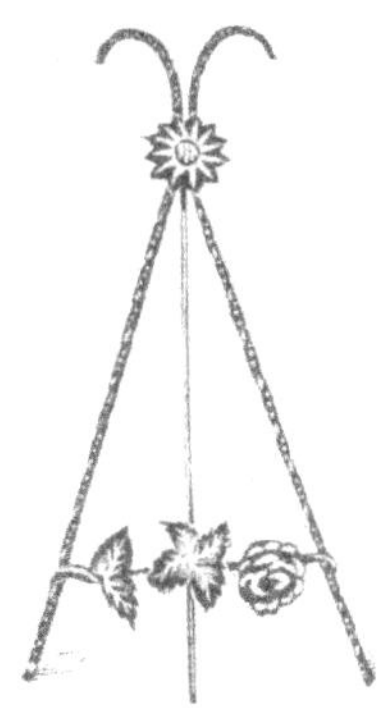

THE CANVAS

He beckoned me over, but I would not go. Instead, I stood in silence and watched. I wasn't sure what it was he was doing, but soon a crowd had gathered. I became curious, and yet I didn't move. His hands were busy, but at what I couldn't tell. He glanced my way again and motioned with his head for me to come. I pretended I didn't see him. Why did he want me to come to him? What was it he wanted me to see?

Others had gathered. He seemed harmless, but I felt some unease. I tried unobtrusively to glance at the expressions of the gatherers, but the distance from the separation of the street made it difficult. I felt his gaze once more and turned to face him. Some in the crowd saw him looking in my direction and they also turned to look at me . . . then another, and another, until all were staring my way.

I slowly crossed the street, as if in a hypnotic state, and walked towards them. All eyes were upon me. Not one altered their stance. It was as though they, too, were hypnotized. In unison, they followed my motion, all in silence. One would have thought their tongues had been removed. I approached—what appeared to be—the back of a canvas.

The man who first beckoned me over walked behind the canvas to greet me. Without saying a word, he took my hand and walked me to the front of the canvas. I don't know why I gave my hand to him, but I did. Still, I had an eerie feeling the crowd was waiting for my reaction—but to what?

I kept my focus on the man and I didn't turn to face the front of the canvas. When he positioned me where he thought I should be, he let go of my hand and gestured for me to look ahead. I was hesitant and stayed my ground. He gestured again, this time with a little more persistence. We were now encircled by those who had gathered—and all remained quiet.

Slowly, I obeyed his command. Turning from him, I looked before me. I'm not sure which came first—the cold chill shivering down my spine, the sweat perspiring from my hands, or the numbness that penetrated every cell within my trembling body.

It was all too surreal. I can't remember what registered first: the woman on the canvas, bearing an identical resemblance to me, and wearing the same clothes I put on that morning—or—the knife she held in her hand, dripping blood on the body that lay at her feet.

WHEN THE BIRDS SING

Sitting in front of the fireplace with her back facing the flames, Barbara felt its warmth radiate through her soul as she had so many times before, and she wondered if she'd have the courage to face another day alone. Sipping the Merlot she held clutched between both hands as though it were the only friend she had, she stared into space, oblivious to the knock on the door.

She felt numb, but her thoughts seeped through and allowed her to reminisce about the tranquil times she and Don had at the end of the day. They'd sit in front of the fireplace, he in his favorite tan recliner and she on the moss rock foot of the fireplace, sipping Merlot and making plans for the summer.

As the knock at the door became more persistent, Barbara was brought back to the moment. "I'm coming," she said in a whisper as she reluctantly got up to answer it. Setting her glass on the end table by the tan recliner, she slowly opened the door as if the effort was more than her frail body could handle.

She gazed upon the tall slender woman standing on the other side of the entryway. The last bright beam of the setting sun was behind the figure, and with its rays shining directly into Barbara's eyes, it took her a couple of seconds to realize that it was her friend, Clair. The look on Clair's face conveyed her shock at seeing the frail, almost lifeless person in front of her. She hardly recognized her. They'd always been so close, and even though she'd called Barbara every few days since Don's death, she hadn't been to see her since the funeral—almost three months ago. Yes, she lived fifty miles away, but was that a good enough excuse to stay away?

As the sun brushed across Barbara's face, Clair saw the pain and sadness in her eyes. She could almost feel it penetrating every cell within her body. *Is this why I stayed away?* she wondered. *Was it easier to be in denial and pretend my friend of twenty years was doing just fine? Did I really believe—knowing her as well as I do—that she wouldn't be suffering?*

"Hello, Clair," said Barbara, breaking the silence. "What are you doing here?" she asked, sounding a little confused. "Is everything all right?"

"Yes, everything's fine," said Clair. "I wanted to see you, I was worried about . . . may I come in?"

"Oh, of course, please come in. It's good to see you, Clair. It's been a while. Would you like a glass of wine, coffee, cup of tea?"

"Coffee would be great," Clair answered as they walked into the kitchen, "but I'll fix it. I know where everything is."

"Okay." Barbara slowly pulled the chair from the table and sat down.

As Clair made the coffee, she could hear the crackling and popping of the last remainders of a fire in the fireplace. She poured the rest of the water in the coffeepot, turned it on, and looked at Barbara. "Isn't it a little late in the season to be having a fire? I realize spring was late in coming this year, but it is the first of May, and the last few days have been beautiful. Are you feeling okay? Are you having chills?" she asked.

"I'm fine. I just wanted a fire. I wanted the routine," she said in a soft voice.

Clair walked over to the table and sat down beside her. "Barbara, when I talk to you on the phone you tell me you're doing fine, but look at you, you're withering away to nothing. It's as though . . ." she stopped.

Barbara shook her head. She could feel the lump forming in her throat. Her eyes began to water. She stared at Clair. "It's as though *what*, Clair? Is it as though I can't get on with my life? What *life*? My life as I knew it is gone. Don took it to the grave with him. Don was my life! Yes, I tell you I'm fine. Isn't that what you want to hear? Isn't it what everyone wants to hear? Then they don't have to feel awkward because they don't know what to say or do—or worse yet, feel guilty, because they're not doing *something*. What can you or anyone else do?"

Clair remained silent and just listened. Barbara continued, "Do you want me to tell you that some days I stay in bed until noon because I don't have the energy to get up, and if I do get up, I don't know what to do with myself? Sometimes I lay awake all night feeling the emptiness on the right side of the bed until it flows over to my side and almost consumes me. There are days I feel nothing; I'm not hungry, I'm not sleepy, I can't think. I stare at the TV, but I don't know what's on. I can't concentrate enough to absorb it." She took a tissue from her pocket and dabbed at her eyes. "Those are some of the better days. The worst are when I can't stop crying, and it hurts so much that I can feel the pain smothering me as though it wants to drain me of the last ounce of life I have—and I wish it would, but it doesn't." She put her hands over her face and sobbed into them.

Clair got up, put her arms around her. "I'm sorry, Barbara, so very sorry." She embraced her a moment longer, and then went to get the coffee. With her back to Barbara, she tried to find the words. "Maybe you're right. Maybe I needed to feel that you were okay. Maybe it was too much like looking in a mirror. If I saw your pain, felt it, I would have to face my own fears."

"What do you mean?"

"I'm forty-eight years old," said Clair. "Jack is sixty-six next week. That's a lot of years between us. Don was only fifty-seven when he had his heart attack. It scared me big-time. I never thought of anything happening to Jack before Don's death. He's in good health, works out, and runs two miles every day. It didn't occur to me that there might come a day when I'd have to face life without him. I wanted to know that you were okay when I called. I guess it reassured me that I would be okay if something happened to Jack." She turned and faced her friend. "Barbara, I know you're going through a difficult time. I want to be here for you, but you have to let your friends in and not pretend you're doing fine. Maybe we haven't insisted on coming over when we should have. Maybe it has something to do with our own fears, or concern of not knowing what to say to you, or not knowing whether you need time alone, or if you really could use some company." She took a deep breath and sighed. "Sometimes it's not easy being on the outside looking in."

"I know I've shut myself off from everyone, especially you, Clair. Of all people, I should be able to reach out to *you*, but it's hard for me to do that. I don't want anyone to feel my pain."

Clair poured the coffee, brought the cups to the table, and set them down. "Don't you see, Barbara—not until you share that pain will you begin to heal."

"I don't know where to begin," said Barbara. I don't know how to start living again. I want to, and more than anything I want this hurt to go away. Clair, I miss him so much! Last week I thought about how Don and I—as soon as spring came—would walk behind the house down to the river, sit on the bench that he built, look for trout to swim by, and listen to the birds sing. The other day I decided to do that. I felt like I was in a daze, and I don't remember seeing any trout swim by. And I didn't hear the birds sing."

Clair reached over and took Barbara's hands into hers. She smiled. "I'm coming over in the morning, and I'll expect you to have the coffee on."

"What are you talking about?"

"You'll see," said Clair as she got up to leave. "We're going to take a walk down by the river."

Barbara walked with Clair to the door, and when she said good-bye, she had a sense that tomorrow was going to be different. She went over to the tan recliner, sat down, and closed her eyes as she stretched out in a reclining position. With arms crossed over her chest, she rubbed her shoulders. Eyes still closed, she could almost feel Don's arms around her, and for the first time since his death, she felt peaceful. And she had hope that when morning came, she'd hear the birds sing.

THE MYSTERIOUS TREE HOUSE

Ginger walked the two miles through the densely rich forest that she'd grown to love over the past ten years. When she first moved to North Carolina, she wasn't thrilled about living in a rural area overpopulated with trees. Her brother Josh, who lived only a mile down the road, talked her into it because he felt she needed to get away from her life in Arizona, and he thought a different environment would be good for her.

Moving from her Phoenix, Arizona neighborhood—where a grocery store, gas station, novelty shops, and restaurants were all within a half-mile radius—was a culture shock, to be sure. However, she needed a change that would get her far away from her abusive ex-husband, Troy, but never in her wildest dreams could she have imagined how quickly she'd adapt to country life. She loved her two-bedroom cabin and the large spacious loft that afforded her room for all her artistic endeavors.

Returning from her walk, she stopped by the creek behind the cabin before going inside. She sat on a large rock overlooking the babbling brook and admired the wildflowers and vegetation. The tranquil scene was cemented in her mind but she never tired of it, and several paintings later, she still found new beauty in its offerings.

"Planning another painting?" Josh said, catching her off guard.

"Josh! You startled me. No, I think I have enough for a while, but each time I sit here I catch something different."

"I can tell, your paintings reflect that."

"The time of day I choose has a lot to do with how they turn out."

"I'm sure it does," he said, and sat down on the rock next to her. "Oh, I almost forgot why I stopped by. Remember the painting you gave me last month? The one I have hanging in my office?"

"The landscape with all the trees?"

"Yes. Well, actually it looks more like a forest. I didn't realize the path you walked was so thick with trees. I guess I've never been that far into the woods—I leave that for my nature-loving sister," Josh teased.

Ginger smiled. "You do realize there never used to be a path. I created one by walking it so much over the last few years. Once in a while I go in a different direction, but not repeatedly like I do that one. So, getting back to the painting . . . what about it?"

"One of the accountants down the hall stopped by my office yesterday to see if I wanted to buy some baseball tickets. Once he saw your masterpiece, he couldn't take his eyes off it. He asked me if he could buy it."

"Really? Wow, that's great! What did you say?"

"I said no, of course. I told him it was a birthday gift from my very talented sister," Josh smiled, "and it wasn't for sale."

"That's exciting! I can't believe someone actually wanted to buy one of my pieces."

"Ginger, I've been telling you for the last two years that you need to market your work. For the life of me, I don't understand why you can't see what an exceptional artist you are. Jerry—the accountant—said he loves trees, and your painting had the best depiction of a forest he'd ever seen. And get this—he asked me if I had any idea what you would charge if he commissioned you to paint one for him."

"Unbelievable! What did you tell him?"

"I told him since I don't delve into the financial aspect of your life, I would have no idea what the cost would be, but considering the accomplished artist that you are, I doubted he could afford you."

Ginger stood from the rock and gave her brother a gentle shove. "Josh, you're full of it! Now tell me what he really said."

Josh laughed, got up and put his arm around his little sister. They looked a lot alike—sandy blond hair, blue eyes, both physically fit, but Josh was eight inches taller than Ginger's five-foot-five frame.

"Let's go inside and continue this conversation over a cold drink," he suggested. They walked up the steps to the back door and Ginger pushed it open.

Noticing she didn't unlock the door first, Josh asked, "Did you leave the door unlocked when you went for your walk today?"

"Yes, I was only gone an hour. I didn't do any sketching or take pictures—just my usual walk."

"Ginger, it doesn't matter whether you're gone an hour, a day, or a week, you need to get in the habit of locking your doors. In this day and age, it's just not safe to keep them unlocked."

"Josh, we live in the boonies—how much safer can you get? You watch too many crime stories! You're becoming paranoid."

"You may be right, but please humor me and lock your doors. I'd feel a lot better." Ginger grunted and poured lemonade in two ice-filled glasses. They sat at the oak table in the kitchen and discussed ways for Ginger to market her talent. Then Josh offered a reasonable, but profitable, price for her first sale to Jerry—should she accept his offer.

"I wish he'd asked for a painting of a creek surrounded by wildflowers, bushes, and trees. I have several of those already done."

"He might go for that, but after seeing the awe in his eyes when he saw the forest on my wall, I think it's only trees he wants. Besides, what else is there to do when you're out there wandering around in the woods? You might as well make yourself useful," he teased.

Painting was a passionate hobby, but Ginger never seriously thought of making money from it. She also enjoyed photography and writing, but painting with acrylics was her first love. She worked from home on the computer as a web designer and her hours were flexible, allowing her time for her creative side.

"Let me think about it over the weekend," said Ginger. "Would the first of the week be soon enough to give Jerry an answer?"

"Sure. Just knowing you're even considering it would thrill him." Josh looked at his watch. "I'd better be getting back. Beth's having the Walkers over for dinner—which reminds me, she said to be sure and invite you. She's making her famous lasagna, and she knows how much you love it."

"That sounds wonderful! Tell her I wouldn't miss it. Thanks, Josh, and thank you for the enticing news about my artwork. You guys are too good to me. One of these Saturday nights, I'll have you and Beth over for dinner. But first, I have to get out of my rut of cooking for one."

"Maybe it's time you thought about dating again. What's it been—two years?"

"Something like that. I think I've come to enjoy my alone time more than I enjoyed dating."

"That's only because you're afraid they'll all turn out like Troy. Most men aren't abusive like your ex-husband. You're forty now—don't you think it's time to trust again?"

"I think it's time for you to leave and get home to Beth," she said, trying to sound stern, then softly added, "If I could find someone as wonderful as my brother, I'd give it a try." She ushered him out the door and he left with a big grin on his face.

Josh was only a few years older than Ginger, but ever since they were kids, he always looked out for her. She knew if she'd been living in North Carolina when she met Troy, she probably wouldn't have married him. Josh would have seen through his subtle controlling ways, and his obvious possessive side that Ginger mistakenly took for love. She was now living close to the brother she adored, and if she ever decided to let her guard down, Josh would be there to offer advice if she needed it.

Putting the empty glasses in the sink, Ginger looked out the window into the woods. She'd already taken her walk that morning, but now she was looking at the forest with renewed interest. She didn't want to paint the exact same scene for Jerry that she painted for Josh, but she knew it would have to be similar. She thought it might be time to venture off and explore a section of the woods where she hadn't been before.

The forest extended for miles, and Ginger was aware of how easy it would be to get turned around in unfamiliar territory. She decided to take a compass—something she hadn't done since she first started enjoying the raw beauty of the woods.

Checking the clock—there was plenty of time to capture new places, take photos, get back in time to shower, and still arrive early for dinner to help Josh and Beth before the Walkers showed up—she grabbed her camera and out the door she went.

Fifteen minutes into her journey, she spotted a rabbit hopping through the trees on her right. She decided to follow, being careful not to frighten him. When he'd stop, she'd pause, making sure to keep a safe distance. He'd sniff around then mosey on his way until he came to a slight opening in the thick of the forest. When Ginger caught up to him, her eyes widened in disbelief. She looked up to see a structure built between two huge maples unlike any tree house she'd ever seen. It curved and angled, nestled in between several of the larger branches. At times it was hard to distinguish whether some of the branches were part of the tree house because they blended in so well. Ginger walked around it then under it, trying to figure out how to get inside. There was a small window on the left side and one on the right side. The door was centered in the middle of two porthole-style windows. A slight ledge went around three sides of the unique structure, but Ginger was bewildered—there was no obvious way to get inside. She didn't see a ladder, steps, or even a rope to climb. Remembering her camera, she quickly started taking photos from all angles, hoping no one would show up before she got through. When she finished, she looked in every direction of the tree house for a sign that someone had been there recently—footprints, food, trash, bushes that might have been disturbed—any recent sign of life, but everywhere she looked, the surroundings were clean and appeared normal. Looking up again, she wondered if someone might be inside. She could tell by its size that it wasn't built as a playhouse for a child but was more likely living quarters for an adult—maybe two.

"Whatcha think of it?"

Ginger was engrossed in studying the tree house and never heard anyone coming up behind her. She flinched and quickly turned around to discover a most unusual character. Standing before her was a woman of average height and build, maybe in her sixties, wearing tattered clothing from head to toe and leaning on a walking stick. Her hair was gray, long, very matted, and in desperate need of a shampoo. Ginger wondered how long it had been since the woman had bathed.

"Do you live here?" asked Ginger.

"What's it to ya?" said the woman. "How did you find this place?" When she spoke, Ginger noticed a missing top right tooth and a center bottom tooth.

"To be honest with you, I followed a rabbit here. I was just taking a walk when I saw a rabbit go in this direction, so I followed him."

"Do you always walk in the woods?"

"As a matter of fact, I do. I'm an artist and I love nature and this is where I get my inspiration." Ginger began to feel uneasy and wondered if there was a man, just like the woman, up in the tree house watching her. She wanted to know more, but she was hesitant to stay and ask questions. "I'm very sorry if

I've upset you by discovering your hideaway. I mean you no harm and I promise—now that I know you're here—not to impose on your privacy again."

"Are you telling me your walks won't take you this way again?" the woman asked sarcastically.

"They never have before. I'm telling you, had it not been for that rabbit, I never would have found this place. In all the years I've been walking these woods, I never knew this was here."

"But you know now, don't you? Do you always walk alone? No husband, no children to walk with you?" She put both hands on the walking stick and pounded it three times on the ground. Ginger could tell she was agitated.

"I can see my presence is disturbing you, and I'm sorry for that. I'll leave you alone and be on my way now."

"You didn't answer my questions."

"Yes, I walk alone," Ginger said, and began walking away.

"No husband, no children?"

"No ma'am—no husband, no children." Ginger thought by answering her, the woman would see that she was harmless.

Once again, Ginger started to leave, but then she saw something moving in the trees. Soon a man appeared, and he was quite the contrast to the woman. He was clean-shaven, nice looking, probably mid-forties, wearing stylish jeans, a blue polo shirt, and a pair of upscale sneakers.

"Auntie Rose, I see you have a visitor," the stranger said. He went up to Ginger and extended his hand. "Hi, I'm Auntie Rose's nephew, Todd." Ginger shook his hand, but before she could introduce herself, Auntie Rose spoke up.

"She's not a visitor. She's an intruder."

"Oh, Auntie, don't be cynical. There are a lot of good people in the world, and she looks friendly to me," he said, giving Ginger a wink and a smile. Auntie Rose mumbled something and walked towards the tree house. "Don't mind my aunt, she's been a hermit too long and doesn't care much for people, except me," he said.

"Nice to meet you, Todd. I'm Ginger," she said, feeling more comfortable and glad that Todd showed up when he did. "Does your aunt live in the tree house?"

"Yes, she does, and has for ten years."

"How does she get in it?"

Todd looked toward his aunt. He could tell she was anxious and he knew she wanted to be alone. "Auntie, go inside. I'll finish up with our guest and be there shortly."

"I'm not putting the stairs down while she's still here."

"Ginger, please turn your back to my aunt." Ginger did as she was told. "See, Auntie, she's not looking, and I'll make sure she doesn't. Now go inside." While Todd made small talk with Ginger, making sure she didn't accidentally turn around, the woman went behind the tree house to the back of the large maple and lifted a branch that was hiding a box built into its trunk. She opened the box, pulled a lever, and down came a flight of stairs. She climbed up; once inside, she pulled a lever by the door and the rope-like stairs disappeared. When she was out of sight, Todd took the opportunity to explain what must have felt like an awkward situation to Ginger.

"This probably seems like some kind of elder abuse to you, since my aunt doesn't look very well taken care of, but I assure you our family has tried, and she's refused all help except from me—which is limited, at best. I seem to be her favorite, mostly because I understand her and I allow her to be herself. And believe me, this is much better than the tent I found her living in after she lost her job and couldn't afford her bungalow anymore."

"Was it difficult for her to find another job?" Ginger asked, wondering how anyone ends up in a tent.

"My aunt has never been comfortable around people. She worked in the back office of a warehouse and didn't have to interact with the other workers—which was perfect for her. When the warehouse decided to go high tech and put all the filing on a computer—which is what my aunt did—they didn't need her anymore. She'd never been on a computer and had no interest in learning. The thought of trying to find another job was too overwhelming. She'd always lived a simple life and was very frugal. Since she didn't socialize, she had money put aside."

Ginger wanted to turn around and see how the woman got up in the tree house but wasn't sure she should. "Is it okay to look now?" she asked.

"Yes, there's no sign of how she got in, but please don't stare. I don't want to make her nervous."

Ginger slowly turned around, looking at the ground first, and then she took a quick peek, only to be disappointed. There was no sign of how the woman entered it.

"What's it like in there?"

"You'd be surprised. I'm an engineer with an interest in creating small sustainable, livable spaces. When I built this for my aunt, I made sure to go as green as possible. She has a biodegradable toilet, a system to catch rainwater, and a battery-powered generator for her small refrigerator, microwave, lights, etc."

Ginger was impressed and wanted to know more. "How does she get the supplies she needs, especially food?"

Before answering, Todd asked Ginger to follow him into the woods. "I don't want my aunt to see that we're still talking. Ginger, you seem like a very nice person, and I feel as though I can trust you, but before I tell you what I'm about to, I'd like to ask that you never come by here again. I believe my aunt to be harmless, but I know she has some issues, and she doesn't like people. She's used to living as a hermit, and to have someone compromise the only way of life she's known for ten years could intensify those issues. I'm hoping you'll understand and respect her need for privacy. I'm also asking that you don't let anyone else know about her situation. I want her to be able to live freely and without fear of strangers."

Ginger thought about it and then replied. "Todd, I understand your concern. I saw how upset I made your aunt just by being here, and I don't see any need for me to come back, so I won't."

"Thank you. Your cooperation is greatly appreciated. Now getting . . . getting back to your question about food and such—well, I take care of that. I make sure she has enough to last a month, but I come by every Saturday to pick up her trash and see what she may be running low on, and then I bring it the following Saturday. And if I'm lucky, about once a month, I'm able to talk her into bathing and washing her hair. I also do her laundry when she lets me, other times she washes the few items she owns in the creek. I've tried buying her new clothes only to find them still in the bag when I return. She's comfortable with what she has."

"I'd say she's very lucky to have you," Ginger said, seeing how much he cared for his aunt.

Todd smiled. "I don't know that she sees it that way. Probably more like a necessary evil she's grown used to—although on a few rare occasions, I actually think she's glad to see me."

Ginger was fascinated by everything Todd had told her and would've liked to have stayed longer, but she was concerned about the time and how much she still had to do before dinner. She explained all this to Todd, but when she shook his hand good-bye, he looked into her eyes, and for a split moment she wasn't sure she wanted to leave.

"Would you mind if I give you my phone number?" he asked. Ginger looked surprised. "I know it must sound strange, but I thought in case you ever come across my aunt wandering in the woods—while you're on one of your walks—you'd give me a call. Granted, she usually stays within her own safe perimeter, but I never know when she might wander."

"Okay, sure."

Todd pulled a business card from his wallet and gave it to her. "My cell number's on there. I can be reached most anytime on that number unless I'm in a meeting or working in my backyard, but I check my messages regularly."

When she took his card, she had a feeling that he would welcome a call from her whether it was about his aunt or not, and to her surprise, it pleased her. She said her good-byes again and began to leave when she realized she wasn't sure which direction to go. She laughed and pulled out her compass.

"I seem to have gotten turned around. I don't think you'll have to worry about me finding this place again," she teased. "Oh, yes, north is that way."

"I'll be going soon also, once I check on Auntie Rose and see to her needs. If you care to wait, I can walk with you and help with directions," he said, smiling. Ginger felt a little embarrassed and assured him that she could find her way, but thanked him for the offer.

On her way back, she paused several times to take pictures of trees that she thought would make a perfect painting for Jerry. By the time she got to the cabin, she realized she had little time to spare before dinner. Quickly grabbing some clothes, she headed for the shower. She couldn't stop thinking about the tree house, amazed at how long it had been there without anyone knowing. But then again, not many people lived close enough to walk the woods like she did.

Stepping out of the shower, she grabbed a towel and began to dry off when she heard a noise outside the bathroom. Thinking it might be Josh or Beth in need of something they forgot to get for dinner that night, she reached for the terry cloth bathrobe she always kept on the back of the door and quickly put it on. Without hesitation, she opened the door only to be confronted by a terrifying sight. She screamed and immediately slammed the door shut, fumbling for the knob to lock it. On the other side stood Auntie Rose without any expression, holding a butcher knife.

"What are you doing in my house?!" yelled Ginger through the door.

"I want to talk to you."

"With a butcher knife?!"

"I don't plan on hurting you, I just want to talk."

"Then why are you holding a knife?" Ginger asked, picking up the pants she'd thrown on the floor. She grabbed her phone to call Josh when Todd's card fell out of the pocket. *Oh, better yet,* she thought. She didn't want to worry Josh when he was having dinner guests, and Todd would know better how to work with his aunt.

"The knife is for my protection in case you want to hurt me."

"This is insane," Ginger mumbled to herself. Shaking, she dialed the number on the card, but it went straight to voicemail. She left Todd a message describing the dire situation and gave her address. She remembered him saying that he checked his messages frequently, so she was hopeful he'd respond quickly. In the meantime, she'd try to reason with Auntie Rose.

"Why would I want to hurt you?"

"Because I wasn't nice to you and you might think I'll be mean."

Ginger began to relax and thought maybe Auntie Rose was telling the truth, and the reason for the knife was because *she* was afraid of what Ginger might do. Todd did tell her that his aunt had issues, but he also said he thought she was harmless. She was tempted to open the door, but she didn't want to be careless in case she was wrong, so she decided to engage in more conversation first.

"I'm still not sure why you want to talk to me. I thought you didn't like people and preferred not to be around them. You certainly gave me that impression," she said through the closed door.

"Todd talked to me after you left. He thinks you're very nice. I don't think he liked the way I treated you. I don't want him upset with me. He's the only one who matters to me. He said he wasn't upset, but I don't believe him. I saw the way he was watching you when you left. I think he'd like to be friends with you, but because of me, he probably won't. Todd is good to me and I don't do anything for him. I know it would make him happy if I was nice to you. I didn't know how you'd act when you saw me, so I brought the knife. I guess that was stupid. All it did was scare you."

Sensing the threat was gone, Ginger began to relax. "May I call you Auntie Rose?"

"No. Only Todd can call me that," she paused. "You can call me Rose."

"Okay. Rose, I'm in a bathroom wearing a bathrobe and I'd like to come out. I'm going to open the door, but first I want to hear you drop the knife. Will you do that?" There was no answer, only silence. Ginger tried again. "Rose, remember what Todd said. He told you I was a nice person. Believe him, because I am. Please drop the knife so I can come out." She put her ear against the door. It was only seconds before she heard the knife clank on the hardwood floor. Unlocking the door and opening it slowly, she peeked out and saw Rose standing stiffly with the knife at her feet. Ginger pointed to the sofa. "Please have a seat over there and I'll come join you. I promise to leave the knife where it is." Once Rose was seated, Ginger carefully walked around the knife and sat on the chair next to Rose.

For the first few seconds they stared at each other in silence. Then Rose folded her hands, placed them on her lap, and lowered her head. Ginger observed her behavior and wondered what she should say. All she knew about this strange woman was that she didn't like to be around people, and according to Todd, she had some issues but he never said what they were. She wanted to be careful with her words. She didn't want to say anything that would cause a negative reaction from Rose.

"Rose, thank you for dropping the knife. I know now that you weren't going to harm me. I hope you know that I mean you no harm, either." Rose slowly raised her head so she could look at Ginger.

"I heard you talking in the bathroom. You called Todd, didn't you?"

"I called him because you frightened me. I didn't know what your intentions were. I didn't know then that you only wanted to talk and didn't mean to scare me. I'll explain that to Todd," she said, hoping to reassure Rose.

"I don't need you to explain me to my nephew. I can do that," she said matter-of-factly and without much emotion.

Ginger kept her voice low and soft. "Yes, you can. I agree, you should be the one to tell him. Rose, you said you wanted to talk to me. Was it because of what Todd said, or was there something else you wanted to say?"

"I don't know. I think when I decided to come here it was to tell you that I'm not a bad person so you would be friends with Todd. I thought if I did that, then I would be doing something nice for him. I only brought the knife in case someone else was here who might want to hurt me. It was only to keep them away from me, not for me to hurt them," she said, and once again lowered her head. "I'm not used to people being nice to me. When I worked in the warehouse, some of them would say hateful things to me, and some were mean. I didn't talk to them. I'd hurry past them so I could get to my office and be alone, because I'd get nervous and sometimes have panic attacks if I had to have a conversation with them. I was okay with a few words, but I didn't like to talk much. Nobody understood. They thought I didn't like them. They thought I was unfriendly."

Ginger knew it had to be difficult for Rose to share that with her. She felt compassion for her. "Rose, I think it took a lot of courage for you to come here, and I think you're very brave to tell me what you did."

Rose lifted her head and looked at Ginger. "Todd was right. You are nice."

Ginger smiled. "I think you are, too. Why don't I make us a cup of tea, and then maybe you'll tell me how you found my home." The kitchen and living room were together in one big open space. She could see Rose and talk to her while she made the tea. Her phone—still in the bathroom—began to ring. She rushed to get it, thinking it was Todd, but it was Josh instead.

"Hi, Josh," she said, wondering what she was going to tell him.

"Hey, is everything okay? I thought you'd be here a little early. The Walkers just arrived and I was getting a little concerned."

"I'm sorry, Josh, I should have called. I lost track of time. I have unexpected company and I won't be able to make it tonight."

"Really? Who? Anyone I know?" he asked, surprised she couldn't have told them that she already had plans.

"Someone I met a while back. They're moving out of state and needed to go over a few things with me that I promised to take care of for them. I completely forgot that tonight was the night they planned to come," she lied. "I'll stop by tomorrow and tell you all about it. Please give Beth my apology and let her know that I do like leftover lasagna."

"Okay. I understand, I guess. We'll miss you. See you tomorrow."

Just as she said goodbye, the tea kettle started whistling. She put the tea bags in the cups, poured the hot water, and noticed Rose was watching her every move.

"I'm sorry for the interruption. That was my brother on the phone. Would you like sugar or honey in your tea?"

"Do you have honey?"

"Yes, I do." Ginger held the bottle up to show her.

"A little of that would be nice."

Ginger put some in both cups and took them into the living room. "Here you go," she said, and handed one to Rose. Rose took a sip and then placed the cup on the coffee table in front of her.

"It tastes good, thank you." Picking up her cup, she looked around the cabin and took another sip, then put it back down again. "Your place wasn't that hard to find. I heard you say north when you left, so I started there. I came up on a pathway and that's when I wasn't sure which way to go, but I guess I made the right decision. When I walked out of the woods there was a creek with a little bridge over it to get to the other side; I walked across it and saw your cabin. I wasn't sure if it was yours. I went up and knocked, but nobody answered."

"I didn't hear a knock," Ginger said, then realized she must've been in the shower.

"The door wasn't locked so I came in. I waited to see if anybody was here. When I didn't see anyone, I walked up to the closed door and then you opened it. It scared me so I held up the knife."

With tremendous relief, Ginger sank back into her chair. "Oh, my gosh, Rose, you really weren't planning on hurting me."

"I might seem unkind at times, but I don't mean anything by it, and I could never hurt anyone. I know I shouldn't have come in, but I thought no one was here. I haven't been in a real home in a very long time. I just wanted to see what it looked like, then I was going to wait outside for you. I never would have taken anything. I know it was wrong and I'm sorry. I don't blame you if you don't believe me."

Ginger leaned forward and smiled. "I do believe you, Rose, and I accept your apology." They were interrupted by loud pounding on the door. Before Ginger could get up, the door burst open and in rushed a frantic Todd, hardly able to contain himself.

"Auntie Rose, what are you doing here?" he said, making his way over to her. Then he saw Ginger in her bathrobe. "Are you okay? Are you hurt? Where's the knife?" Rose pointed to it. He looked at the knife on the floor, then back to his aunt and Ginger who both appeared calm. Then he noticed the teacups. It certainly didn't look like a dire situation, as Ginger had indicated in her message. "Someone please tell me what's going on here."

"We're having a cup of tea. Would you like one?" said Auntie Rose as if nothing had ever happened.

Ginger began to laugh, she couldn't help herself. The scene was too bizarre, and she could only imagine how it appeared to Todd after the concern and panic he must've felt hearing her voicemail. She went over to him, took his hand, and led him to the sofa.

"I think you'll need to sit for this, but I assure you, everything's okay. Your aunt has a lot to tell you. I'll share some things with you when she finishes."

Todd looked at his auntie and waited. Soon she began telling him everything that had transpired. Todd listened intently. To think of the aunt that he knew—even being capable of showing up at Ginger's was one thing, but bringing a butcher knife was inconceivable. By the time she was through, he was more understanding and grateful she hadn't intended to hurt Ginger. Then Ginger gave her view of what happened, emphasizing that she believed Rose to be harmless.

"Ginger, I'm sorry you had to endure such a frightening experience. I can't even imagine what it must have been like for you. I admire your ability to work through a difficult and scary situation and come through it with such compassion and understanding. You're a very special person."

"Thank you. I would never want to go through that again, but I'm thankful for the end result. I think Rose made some major strides today. She talked to me and we had tea together." She looked at Rose and smiled and then another significant breakthrough occurred—just when Todd thought he'd heard and seen everything—Rose smiled back.

"Auntie Rose, I think it's time for us to leave," he said, looking at Ginger in her bathrobe. "Ginger, I hope you'll still have time to enjoy any plans you might have for the evening."

"I was only going to my brother's house for dinner, but I told him something came up and I'd see him tomorrow." She walked them to the door. Todd hesitated as if he didn't want to leave.

"Ginger, once I get Auntie Rose settled, I'd like to come back and take you to dinner. It's the least I can do for all you've been through. Besides, you missed dinner at your brother's and you have to eat," he said with a grin.

"I'd like that, Todd, and I promise I'll be a little more presentable."

He smiled. "I see nothing wrong with the way you look, but I guess the restaurant might frown on bathrobes."

"Does this mean you two are friends?" asked Rose.

"I hope so, Auntie Rose."

"Rose, I think you may have gotten your wish," Ginger said with a smile.

"Well, if this means you're going to be friends, you better start calling me Auntie Rose. Now let's go, Todd. I want to get home so I can take a bath and wash my hair."

A Day at the Office

Beverly came to work that morning with no expectations of what the day would bring. The buzz was that a change had been made in upper management. Having heard this before, she gave little credence to the rumor. She was sure something needed to change but what, she didn't know.

Morale had been steadily declining in the past year until it reached its present stagnant state. The office environment was more like a robotic arena. Everyone moving around—doing what was expected, no more, no less—without much emotion or enthusiasm, seemingly prewired in hopes of not running down before the end of the day.

Beverly thought how symbolic this was of her own life, just going through the motions and merely existing. Little did she know that it all was about to shift gears.

As she sat in her open cubicle, wondering if any management change had taken place, she amused herself by conducting a mental character study of the zombie-like figures encompassing the secretarial pool. She knew it was Monday because Barbara Miller was wearing her usual Monday outfit, and every Tuesday, she'd wear the same clothes she had on the previous Tuesday, etc. *How boring!* thought Beverly. She glanced over at Rachel Cox, the wannabe actress dressed in a miniskirt and tight sweater, looking as though a movie producer would walk in any moment and discover her. She had on makeup so heavy it would do a clown proud. "If only she knew how ridiculous she looked," whispered Beverly to herself.

"Have you heard the news?" came the excited voice of Cyndie Weber, startling Beverly back to reality.

"I haven't heard anything. What're you talking about?"

"You haven't seen him? He's gorgeous!"

"Who?"

"The new manager! Old man Bickman is finally out."

"How do you know this?" asked Beverly, a little skeptical of Cyndie's exuberance. After all, Cyndie was the only one left who still managed to have a cheerful attitude on a daily basis.

"I was passing by the conference room when Mr. Scarborough and this incredible-looking man came walking out," explained Cyndie. "They almost bumped into me. 'Cyndie,' Mr. Scarborough said, 'I'd like you to meet Chad Maxwell. Chad will be replacing Melvin Bickman as manager of the claims department. He'll be a great asset to Norwest Insurance Company.' I'm telling you, Beverly, I couldn't take my eyes off him. If he can't bring some excitement to this place, no one can."

Beverly gave her a dubious look. She wondered if anyone, or anything, could bring excitement to the claims department of an insurance company.

"He's probably a self-indulgent, conceited, ego-powered tyrant."

"Oh, and you'd rather have boring Mr. Bickman? Wait until you meet him and then tell me what you think," retorted Cyndie, glowing as she walked back to her cubicle.

"Some people are easily impressed," mumbled Beverly as she shuffled the stack of papers on her desk, wondering how and when she'd allowed herself to become so cynical. Remembering the positive, fun-loving person she used to be, she realized the trials of the past couple of years had left their mark. After only two years of marriage, the man she thought would be by her side forever left her for another woman. A year later, a truck driver killed the childhood friend who was always there for her through all her highs and lows. When he only got probation, Beverly was furious. Before long, she'd built a protective cocoon around her emotions—especially when it came to men.

"I believe you must be Beverly Parker," said the masculine voice as he approached her desk. She looked up to see what she'd always imagined a Greek god would look like. "I'm . . . "

"Yes, I know who you are," she said, interrupting him. "You're Chad Maxwell, the new manager." Beverly felt confident that Cyndie's description, as well as her own observation, would prove her correct.

"I am," he said with a smile, flashing a perfectly aligned set of white enamel. "Bob Scarbough," he continued, "told me to see you first. He said, having been here the longest, you would be the most helpful in showing me around."

I bet he did! And I bet you're wondering how long it will take me to be captivated by your charm. Like I have nothing better to do, she thought. With an air of indifference, she replied, "Yes, Mr. Maxwell, I will be happy to do that, but I hope you won't mind if I finish this report first."

"Please, call me Chad. I like working in an informal environment and, yes, of course you may finish your report. I didn't mean to imply that you were to stop what you were doing. Let me know when it's convenient. I'm in no hurry. I'll just be in my office putting the rest of my things away. It's been nice meeting you, Beverly."

"It's been nice meeting you also, Mr. uh . . . Chad. I'll see you shortly." She began busying herself with work that she knew could have waited.

Watching him walk towards his office, she was a little disarmed by his genuine warmth and down-to-earth demeanor. However, there was little time to think about that first impression. Within seconds of his departure, Beverly's desk was flooded by amateur gossip columnists wanting information.

Barbara Miller, Cyndie Weber, and Rachel Cox were all speaking at once. "What was he like?" "What did he say?" "Is he as nice as he looks?" "Did he discuss any future plans?" "What did you think of him?"

"Please, everyone, settle down! Listen to yourselves, you sound like a bunch of teenagers! He was here all of five minutes, there's nothing to report."

"Come on, Beverly, admit it. You must've had at least a mild hormone rush when you first laid eyes on him," said Rachel.

"He's here to do a job, and so are we. I haven't time to pay attention to how he looks. What's important is what he can bring to this company."

"I'd say he's bringing an awful lot," laughed Barbara. "In the last few minutes, his presence alone has brought more energy to this building than we experienced all of last year."

"Okay, enough already," scolded Beverly. "Let's get back to work. You'll have the opportunity to meet him . . . Chad, that is . . . later. I suggest you put on your professional hats."

"I'll put on or off anything he'd like," giggled Rachel, strutting her body across the aisle.

"Let's go, Cyndie, and leave Beverly in her own private rut," said Barbara as they walked back to their cubicles.

Looking down the hall, Beverly could see the door to Chad's office. Wondering what he might be doing, she knew enough time had lapsed: It was time to show him around. As she was getting up from her desk, she noticed a small-framed man, probably in his late thirties, approach Chad's office. He didn't go in. He just stood there, fidgeting with something in his pocket. She watched him pace back and forth and then put his hand on the doorknob, but he still didn't go in. He released his grip and once again began to pace. The man seemed distraught, so Beverly decided to see if she could help. With his right hand in his coat pocket, head down, he continued to pace. His back was towards her as she approached.

"Excused me, may I . . . "

Startled, the man turned around, grabbed her arm, and barged into Chad's office. As he pulled a gun from his pocket, he pushed Beverly over to where a shocked Chad was standing. Waving the gun nervously at both of them, he asked Chad, "Are you Melvin Bickman?"

"No, I'm not," replied Chad.

"I was told this was his office."

"If you have a problem with Mr. Bickman, you're a day late. He no longer works here."

"Are you the person responsible for paying claims?" asked the man, trembling to the point of having to hold the gun with both hands.

"I suppose I am," replied Chad in a calm voice. There was something so fragile about the intruder that Chad decided to try reasoning with him, hoping—even if not intentionally—the gun wouldn't go off. "Sir, I'm Chad Maxwell. I'm taking over for Mr. Bickman. Please tell me why you're here and maybe I can help."

Numb, Beverly just stood there listening to their exchange as she watched the stranger's shaking hands around the piece of metal. The reality of the situation had not yet fully registered.

The man began pacing and shaking his head, glancing back and forth between Chad and Beverly. "I just wanted to give them a decent burial. I didn't want any money for myself. When it happened, I had been out of work for six months, but I paid my premium before the grace period was up. Bickman said he never got my check. I know he got it because it cleared the bank. All I wanted to do was give my family a proper burial.

"I'm not sure what you're talking about, but I don't think you want to hurt anyone. Please give me the gun," said Chad, extending his hand.

The distraught stranger stared at Chad and Beverly for what seemed like an eternity. Finally, he slumped to his knees and dropped the gun. Chad quickly picked it up and told Beverly to call the police.

"The gun isn't loaded," the man said. "I couldn't harm anyone, but I know you have to call the police. I don't care what happens to me, all I want is for my wife and little girl to be buried with dignity."

"Please come over here and sit down," Beverly suggested, pointing to a chair by Chad's desk. "Tell us what happened to your family."

Taking Beverly's advice, he sat down and, with tears in his eyes, began to tell his story. "A couple of months ago on a Friday afternoon, my wife picked up our daughter from preschool. They were on their way home when an uninsured drunk truck driver ran them off the road. The car went down an embankment and rolled over and over before hitting a tree. They were killed instantly."

This was all too familiar for Beverly and brought back painful memories. "What is your name?" she asked.

"Kenneth Dole. I'm sorry if I frightened you, but I was desperate. They've been holding my wife and daughter in that cold room for two months while I tried to come up with the money to bury them. I couldn't get through to Bickman and he never returned my calls. A copy of my cleared check is in my pocket. I was going to prove to him that my policy was in force."

"Must we call the police? He's obviously harmless. Can't we keep this between ourselves?" Beverly pleaded.

"What did you say your name was?"

"Kenneth Dole."

Chad walked over to his desk and opened the drawer. He pulled out a piece of paper in the form of a check. "I found this when I was putting my things away. It's a check made out to Kenneth Dole."

"My check!"

"This is why Bickman is no longer here," Chad whispered to Beverly. "Bob Scarborough discovered that Bickman had a drinking problem and the claims department was in turmoil."

Kenneth Dole looked at Chad. "Mr. Maxwell, if I'm incarcerated, would you take this check and see that my family is taken care of?"

"I think you've been through enough, Mr. Dole. I won't call the police if you can make me a promise."

"Anything, what is it?"

"Promise you will get some counseling. I know a couple of good therapists specializing in grief counseling, and if you'd like, I would be happy to set up your first appointment. And one more thing, Mr. Dole—no more guns. They never solve anything."

"I'd appreciate it if you'd set the appointment with the therapist," he said holding back tears, "and I promise you, I'll be there. As for guns . . . you have my word. I hope I never have to look at another gun. Thank you! Thank you both!"

Beverly gave a sigh of relief, turned to Chad, and smiled. "I think I'm going to enjoy working with you, Chad Maxwell.

Murder on the High Seas
Cabin 354

It was the second day at sea of my fifteen-day cruise. I was in the Piazza enjoying coffee and an almond croissant when the loudspeaker came on.

"This is your Captain speaking. All guests return to your stateroom immediately! I repeat, return to your stateroom now! This is not a drill, the ship is not in an emergency situation, but I need you to return to your quarters and wait for further instructions. More information will be forthcoming when everyone is in their rooms and accounted for. I repeat: The ship is not in danger. We're investigating an incident, and in order to understand what has happened, it's imperative that all guests return to their cabins. I apologize for the inconvenience and appreciate your cooperation. I will give an update as soon as possible," he said.

Well, that was quite different, I thought as I observed my surroundings, expecting chaos to erupt. But instead, people were moving slowly. Were they in a state of shock, I wondered, or just trying to process the Captain's message like I was? The crew appeared calm as they encouraged everyone to return to their rooms.

I'm a seasoned cruiser and, although I was bewildered by what the Captain said, I assumed that whatever the concern was it would be resolved quickly. I also assumed that those more panicked than the rest of us—running up to crew members, questioning everything, especially if it was safe to get on the elevators—were probably first-time cruisers.

Most of my experiences at sea were pleasurable and uneventful, although there was the time on an Alaskan cruise when the ocean was tumultuous—forty-foot waves slammed against the ship—and half the passengers got sick. Some were vomiting in the hallways as they stumbled back to their rooms. If you hadn't been drinking, you felt like you had. The ship bounced from side to side, making it quite difficult to walk. By morning, all was calm, but it was an evening to remember.

I finished my croissant, grabbed my coffee—which was in a to-go cup because it stays hotter, and I like it that way—and joined the remaining passengers to return to my cabin. I heard a lot of speculation about what was going on, such as: "Someone must've fallen overboard," said one. "No," said another, "they would have yelled, 'man overboard!'" And then there was the obvious thought—an outbreak of a highly contagious disease, like Covid. In the midst of all this, I heard my name being called.

"Jasmine! Jasmine!" called the voice.

I turned and saw a man who looked familiar, but at the moment I couldn't place him. The frown on my forehead gave me away.

"It's Steve from the piano lounge," he said.

"Steve? Oh, yes, I remember now." *How could I have forgotten,* I thought, remembering how he intruded on my space—which annoyed me terribly at first. He wanted to talk and I wanted to listen to the piano player, who was quite good and the reason there were few empty chairs. Steve took the one next to me. I was sitting directly in front of the piano at a table for two when he asked if the seat was vacant. I hesitated at first—wanting to say no, that the seat would be occupied shortly by my husband, but of course that would've been a lie. I was traveling alone. Traveling alone does have its advantages, but eventually you do get tired of talking to yourself. When the piano player took his fifteen-minute break, it was then that I realized, to my surprise, that I was fully engaged in the conversation with Steve.

"I imagine you meet a lot of different people and one face blurs into another," he said, "being a writer and all," he added as the elevator opened, and together we got on.

I studied him and smiled. "Sorry for the delay in my recall, but I was caught up in the moment, like everyone else, and quite removed from the piano lounge. If I remember correctly, you said you were a freelance journalist—not exactly sure what that means, except that you probably meet a lot of different people also." Before he could respond, the elevator stopped on the ninth floor—Dolphin deck—and the door opened.

"This is where I get off," he said, holding the door, "but if this issue gets resolved before tonight—which I suspect it will—maybe I'll see you in the lounge later."

"Maybe," I said when he exited. The Dolphin deck is on the ninth floor and I was on the fourteenth floor—Baja.

By the time the elevator got to Baja deck, I was the only one left. Lingering in the Piazza as I did, allowed for most of the other passengers to return to their rooms before me. I welcomed not having to navigate my way through the crowd. My room was a few corridors down from the elevators, and I made two turns along the way. I didn't see any of the crew, and it was very quiet until I approached my room. At the end of the hall, I saw someone coming out of a cabin—which was strange, since we were told to stay until further notice—and he was soon followed by two men pushing a gurney with what looked to be a body on it. I quickly slipped into my room so as not to be seen. After all, if he was sickened, I didn't want to get too close. And if a crime had occurred, I didn't want someone thinking I might've seen something.

"That must be the emergency!" I said out loud, as if I were speaking to someone. I've often wondered if other people living alone speak their thoughts. I don't know why I do, except if it seems important, hearing my thoughts keeps me focused. It's as though having a rambling conversation with myself helps to make sense of it all.

"A body is wheeled out of a room," I continued out loud. "There's a sheet over him—the body seemed large, so I'll assume it's a man for now. I couldn't tell if the sheet was pulled over his head. Was he seriously ill and being taken to the infirmary, or was he deceased? If deceased, what caused it? Was it a heart attack or a mysterious illness?"

We had a couple more sea days before arriving at our first port in Hawaii. I've been on ships when a medical emergency occurred, and if we weren't in port, then a helicopter would come and take the individual to the nearest hospital. *Hmm . . . can't be that,* I thought. If that were the case, then there'd be no reason for the Captain to deliver the message he gave this morning. It would be handled quietly and without incident. There'd be no need to involve the rest of the passengers. But the Captain was concerned about something, enough to have all of us go back to our cabins, so what does that mean? Could it be a deadly quick-spreading disease? What if someone was murdered? I'm not sure how that would be handled, since I've never been on a ship when that's occurred. Worse yet, what if more than one person was murdered? Do they suspect a serial killer among us? Is that why the Captain wanted everyone back in their rooms? *Makes sense. They could keep everyone safe while they reviewed the passenger list, looking for someone who stands out.* Okay, now I'm allowing my imagination to go too far—or am I? Stranger things have happened, like the man on his honeymoon who was found dead from a suspicious fall over a balcony—the media reported about it for weeks.

I remember a time years ago when I was on a cruise that I'd earned with my company. Back then, they didn't scrutinize passengers as thoroughly as they do now. After we'd returned to the ship from a full-day excursion, we had just enough time to get ready for dinner. One woman in our group couldn't be accounted for and she didn't show up for dinner. Our manager became concerned and checked with her roommate to see if she was sick, but she was told that she never came back to the room. "Maybe she wasn't hungry and decided to go to the early show instead," said the roommate. "That could be," said the manager, "but it would've been nice to let someone know." No one thought much of it after that, but when she didn't show up for breakfast, our manager got the Captain involved. We wondered if she was left ashore, or accidently fell overboard. Turns out that this middle-aged mother of four spent the night with a twenty-something steward in his room. I guess they were discovered when the cabin steward didn't show up the next morning to clean his assigned cabins.

Since traveling solo, I notice I'm paying more attention to people and my surroundings than I ever did before. Like in the Piazza this morning, I panned the room observing couples who obviously enjoyed being together; then there were those who I surmised were hoping a cruise might remind them of what brought them together in the first place. Now that I think about it, I don't remember seeing anyone that stood out as being odd or someone to be concerned about.

This cruise is comprised mostly of seniors, possibly because it's fifteen days long, and it might be too expensive for younger couples, families, or too difficult for some to leave their jobs for two weeks.

I don't know what the average age is for a criminal—or murderer, for that matter—but if either has caused the emergency on board, I feel the eighty-plus age bracket can be ruled out. Many in this age group are in wheelchairs or need the help of a walker or cane. And I don't believe the healthier ones would have the speed to get away quickly from the scene of a crime—assuming a crime has been committed. There's still the chance that it could be a highly contagious disease, and by having us all return to our cabins, it would make it easier to invoke a mandatory quarantine. And by having everyone return to their rooms, it would also make it easier to locate a missing person—although I did see that body on the gurney being wheeled out of a cabin down the hall from me. Could he be the victim of a deadly disease, murder, or even attempted murder from a robbery gone bad? I'm sure there are wealthy people on this ship who carry a lot of cash and expensive jewelry with them when they travel. Did the perpetrator know the victim? That would explain how he gained access into his cabin. Or could it be a member of the crew delivering a complimentary fruit tray?

As a mystery writer, there are times that I tend to go out on a limb. But I'm sure there are wilder stories than mine being conjured up by confused travelers, and they didn't see what I saw.

Static came over the loudspeaker, then a male voice. "This is your Captain, and I have important information. Please mute your TVs so you can hear me clearly. We have a passenger who's passed away and there are indications that foul play might be involved. We have contacted the officials in Oahu, and they will be aiding us in this investigation once we dock in Honolulu. While at sea for the next two days, we will be conducting interviews with passengers in hopes of gaining insight into what might have happened to this individual. Since we are not sure if this is an isolated situation or why it has happened, we are advising caution when moving around the ship, and recommend that families stay together. The ship will operate in a normal capacity with all restaurants, shops, and entertainment available to guests. Under the circumstances, if anyone would feel more comfortable—especially if you're traveling alone—to have your meals in your room, all room service fees will be waived.

"I want to emphasize that we will be doing everything necessary to ensure your safety, but we also need you to be vigilant. If you overhear or see anything suspicious, bring it to our attention immediately by alerting one of the crew. When we arrive in Honolulu, you will not be able to disembark until the ship has been cleared by the authorities. I will have further information on that closer to docking time.

"Thank you. That's all for now."

Here I am, by myself, no one with me to move safely around the ship. I could stay in my room or go out on the balcony and enjoy the vast ocean, but eventually I'd have to come back in . . . and then what? Do I wait until I hear voices in the hallway, or assume I'll be fine and walk to the elevator alone? Considering the culprit knows they're looking for him, he might not act again. I ponder both thoughts.

Being a mystery writer doesn't clothe you in bravery, but it has made me more skeptical, curious, and suspicious. During times like these, I wish I could take on the role of one of my characters, knowing all will end well. But in real life, it doesn't always happen that way.

I thought about what the Captain said, and I felt there was probably a lot more that he didn't say, but he did what he needed to do. He alerted the passengers to a death that could've been caused by foul play but avoided words like; murder, killer, dangerous person. He needed to establish calm and, at the same time, make sure each person understood the need to be cautious. It was a balancing act, and I felt he did it well.

"Okay, Jasmine, let's get out of here," I said, looking in the mirror at myself. I paused to reflect on the woman staring back at me. Not bad, I thought, for a middle-aged fifty-two-year old. I've always looked younger than my years, and I keep reasonably active, which helps prevent my waistline from expanding. I always wanted to be taller, with long, sexier legs, but 5' 6" isn't too bad. My Italian mother and Greek father love to cook, and they're good at it. I live close to my parents, and since I don't like to cook, I pop in at mealtime at least once or twice a week, so I'm always fighting an extra five pounds, but it doesn't seem to affect how my clothes fit.

I do like my hair. It has just enough natural curl to keep it wavy all the way to my shoulders. If I'm having a bad hair day, I pull it back into a ponytail, or a bun. I keep it a dark chestnut color—with help from a bottle—and that goes well with my brown eyes.

I grab my crossbody purse containing my reading glasses, room key, lipstick, lip gloss, and tissues for my allergies, and throw it over my head. There's also a place for my phone, but most of the time I keep it in my right pants pocket. You don't really need a purse while on the ship because any purchases or services—like in the salon or gift shop—are added to your onboard account and settled before you leave. Not knowing how long I'd be out of my room, it was easier to take the purse and not have to go back for reading glasses or extra tissues. The purse is a blue-and-white quilted material and lightweight so it's not cumbersome to carry. I like it, but today not so much. It doesn't go with my tan capris and pink shirt. Oh, well . . . here I go.

The hallway was quiet, almost eerie. I walked down the first corridor then the second without seeing anyone, although I sensed someone was nearby. I rounded the corner to the elevators and still, no one in sight. *Had they already gone down or were they afraid to leave their room?* I wondered. I was on the port side of the ship, but I didn't see or hear anyone coming from the starboard side either.

It seemed to take longer for one of the elevators to open—which was a good sign—meaning they were probably in use and guests were getting out of their rooms. When the door opened, it was empty. I stepped in and pushed #5. Just as the door started to close, two hands appeared and pushed the doors open.

"Oh, I'm sorry," I exclaimed, "I didn't see you or I would've held the door." He stepped in without uttering a word and he didn't push a floor to get off, which made me a little nervous. Of course, deck five could've been where he planned to get off, and it was already selected. He reminded me of a defensive football player turned biker. He was large and muscular with tattoos across his neck and running down both arms. He stood still, looking stoic. I didn't know if he was just thinking about what he was going to do or if he had something more menacing on his mind. We skipped floors twelve and eleven but stopped on deck ten. To my relief, he got off. I did find it strange that he never pushed a button for any floor, but got off on ten. Thankfully, a family and two couples got on, and I found myself relaxing. The family got off on seven, where some of the shops were, and the couples got off on deck five with me.

When there wasn't a specific place that I wanted to be, I usually ended up in the Piazza, especially if there was entertainment. To me, it is the heart of the ship. There's a big open area in the center with open staircases at each end going up to the sixth and seventh floors. On one side of center is where the musicians perform. The entertainment can either be an individual on steel drums, violin, guitar, or a trio performing. Guests can dance in the center, but that usually happens at night. Depending on the ship, the perimeter surrounding the center has tables and chairs for two to four people. And next to that are an open bar, coffee shop, and a twenty-four-hour international café, where you can get breakfast items in the morning and sandwiches and salads later. On the other side is usually where the ice cream or gelato can be found. I like the openness of the Piazza and watching people come and go, and I like to go down in the morning and get a cappuccino and an almond croissant. Sometimes I find an empty table by the window, and I'll sit there so I can look out at the ocean.

I decided to find a table and then order a drink. My eyes were focused towards the window when I heard my name being called. To my right was a table for four, and Steve was sitting there with another man and a woman.

"Jasmine, come join us," he said. Being with other people sounded more inviting than sitting alone by the window, so I went over and sat in the empty chair by Steve.

Steve introduced me to Jack and Barb, a retired couple from Florida. It's not uncommon for people to ask if they can sit with you when you have empty chairs at your table. It's a nice way to meet people, especially if you're by yourself.

We chatted about the usual stuff—where we were from, why we liked to cruise, and how often we did, and then Barb asked if I was traveling alone. "I am," I said. "I've been divorced for five years and I've gotten used to traveling solo."

"That's very brave of you," said Barb. "As much as I enjoy cruising, I don't think I could do it by myself." She studied me a moment, then added, "But of course, you're a lot younger than I am." She probably thought I was in my forties rather than early fifties, but either way, I was younger. I'm not good at guessing someone's age, but Barb and Jack looked to be in their mid-to late-seventies.

"I'd imagine, being alone and all, that the Captain's message might be more of a concern for you than the rest of us," said Jack.

"Do you think that because I'm a woman traveling alone, or do you also feel that way about Steve since he's traveling alone?" I asked with a bite in my tone. Under the circumstances, Jack's question was reasonable, but my answer wasn't, and I could tell that I made him uncomfortable. I've been known to overreact when compared unequally to a man, but in this situation, I was being ridiculous. I'm sure that Steve—who looked to be between 6' to 6' 2" probably late fifties and physically fit—wouldn't have felt as uneasy as I did on my way to the elevator. "That's a fair question, Jack. I'm not overly concerned, but I'm sure if I had to, I wouldn't be able to fight someone off as easily as Steve could," I said, hoping to put Jack at ease.

"The Captain wasn't very clear about what happened, other than foul play. What exactly does that mean?" asked Barb. I looked to Steve—since he was a journalist, I thought maybe he could offer some insight.

"Foul play can mean different things, depending on the situation. If it was accidental or a brawl had occurred, then I don't believe the Captain would have mentioned foul play," said Steve.

"The ship has cameras, so I think they'll figure out who did this by the time we dock in Honolulu," Jack said.

Barb chimed in. "I wonder where on the ship it happened. It seems—other than our cabins—the only place without cameras would be in the restrooms."

"If it happened there, the next person going into the bathroom would have discovered the body—unless it was left in a stall and not found until the bathroom was cleaned. Then I think it might be more difficult to determine who did it," said Jack.

"Jack and I were on the balcony and we might've missed part of the Captain's message before coming inside. Did he say whether it was a man or a woman?"

"No, Barb, he didn't," said Steve. "What do you think, Jasmine—any thoughts?"

I wasn't sure what I wanted to add to the conversation, but for some reason I didn't want to mention what I'd seen going to my room. Jack and Barb were pretty sharp individuals and seemed to be very nice, harmless people—as did Steve—but I really didn't know them. I wasn't sure who I could trust, so I didn't want to say anything about seeing a body being removed from cabin 354 on deck fourteen. *What if they repeated what I said to someone else, or the wrong person overheard them?* I thought. And eventually, as rumors go, the facts would be distorted, and it could end up being that I saw a person coming out of cabin 354, possibly the killer. If that fell on the wrong ears, I could be viewed as a witness to the crime.

I smiled and said, "I tend to get myself into trouble when I speculate too much, so I'm keeping my thoughts a blank canvas until the Captain gives more information." Actually, I had all kinds of scenarios running through my head, but I didn't want to share them.

"Jasmine, your rings are beautiful and look to be quite expensive," Barb said, looking at my hands. "Maybe until this matter on the ship is resolved, you might want to keep them in the safe in your room."

I hadn't given any thought to the value of my rings, but Barb made a very good point. We don't know why the victim encountered foul play. Each of my rings has a special meaning, and that's why I wear them. I don't wear them because they're valuable. The three diamond and emerald rings I inherited from my grandmother. I never gave any thought to their value, but I do remember how much she loved expensive rings. My aunt on my mother's side—who was like a second mother to me—left me her antique diamond dinner ring when she passed away from a massive heart attack. Once I started wearing them, I realized how much I enjoyed rings, and on two different occasions I bought a diamond ring for each pinkie.

"Thanks for the advice, Barb," I said, looking down at my hands. "These are family heirlooms and I never take them off, even when I sleep. But under the circumstances I probably should be more careful and not wear all of them at once."

"Well, Barb," said Jack, "let's go look through the shops before dinner." He stood up and looked at Steve and me. "It's been nice visiting with you folks."

"I enjoyed meeting you both," said Barb. "Maybe we'll run into each other again." Steve and I echoed the sentiments. I'd forgotten about ordering a drink, and Steve waved someone over.

"What would you like, Jasmine?" asked Steve.

"Chardonnay, please."

The server looked at Steve. "And you, sir, would you like another Coke?" he asked.

"Yes, but make it rum and Coke this time."

I'd forgotten that I put the daily activity sheet in my purse until Steve asked what I was going to do after dinner. I pulled it out and looked at my options.

"I think I'll go to the show in the theater tonight. They're doing a tribute to the Beatles. It sounds like fun. What about you?" Our drinks arrived before Steve could answer. I glanced around the room while the drinks were being set down and I saw the man from the elevator. He sat at a table close to the window facing Steve's back. For a moment, he seemed focused on me, but then he turned and looked out the window. I shuddered, and Steve noticed.

"You okay?" he asked.

"Don't turn around, but there's a man sitting behind you who was on the elevator with me, and for some reason he makes me uncomfortable."

"What did he say to you to make you feel that way?"

"Nothing. He said absolutely nothing, but I thought it was odd that he didn't choose a floor, and then he got off on the first one the elevator stopped at. I didn't see him anywhere when I got on the elevator, but just as the doors were closing, there he was."

"The elevators do ding when they're approaching, so maybe he was coming out of his room, heard it ding, and rushed to get there in time," Steve offered.

"You're probably right, and under normal circumstances I might not have given it much weight. But considering that someone's died on this ship, and we don't know how or by whom, I seem to be questioning everything. I wish we knew how he died. It had to be by strangulation or poison. It would be almost impossible to get a gun on board."

"You would think, but stranger things have happened," said Steve, taking his last swallow. "I wonder where it happened?"

I didn't mention it occurred on my floor, or that I later walked down and saw that it was cabin 354. Steve was very friendly, and I didn't want him to feel that he had to look out for my safety.

I looked at my watch. "I've enjoyed the company, but it's getting close to dinnertime and I want to go back to the room and change clothes." I smiled. "I'm sure we'll run into each other again."

"Jasmine, is the man from the elevator watching you?"

I looked, and then scanned the area. "No, he's gone! How did he leave without me seeing him?" Steve turned around, but there was no one sitting behind him.

"A lot of people have been coming and going, he must've gotten caught up in the flow. Would you like me to walk with you to your room?"

"Thank you, but that's not necessary. If it was late at night, and no one was around, I might take you up on your offer. I see people heading towards the elevators so I'm not concerned," I said. As I got up to leave, Steve asked me about the show.

"Jasmine, would you mind if I join you in the theater tonight? The show sounds interesting and I'd enjoy sitting next to someone who—I somewhat know—rather than a total stranger. I don't want to intrude, and if you prefer going by yourself, I understand." I told him I didn't mind, and we made plans when to meet.

I met Steve outside the theater doors promptly at 7:15. The show started at 7:30, and the theater was almost packed. We sat in the back close to the exit doors. We made small talk while waiting for the show to begin, and I think it was the first time that I really paid attention to how Steve looked. He was smartly dressed in a gray shirt and black slacks, and I noticed he was wearing cufflinks. I can't remember when I last saw someone wearing cufflinks—especially on a cruise ship—unless it was in the dining room on formal night. He reminded me of an old English professor I once had, same salt-and-pepper hair and potted face from acne long gone.

Steve seemed to be enjoying the show, and I was totally into it—the singers were fantastic! Then, about midway through the show, something awful happened. The singer representing John Lennon was singing "Imagine"—my favorite Beatles song—when all of a sudden, he collapsed and started convulsing. Then he suddenly stopped and just laid there. The stage manager came running out and knelt down beside him. He put his head on his chest, took his pulse, then looked up at the concerned cast members. Forgetting that the singer's mic was on, he said he couldn't feel a pulse and instructed someone to call the medics. Hearing all this, the audience let out a gasp, and the stage curtains were immediately closed. Before anyone could address the audience, Steve grabbed my arm.

"Let's get out of here," he said. Without even thinking, I followed Steve's lead.

As we were walking away from the theater, it hit me, and I found it strange. I stopped and looked at Steve. "Isn't it unusual for a journalist to walk away from a potential story?"

"What story?" he said. "Someone will address the audience and say that the singer had a seizure and is being taken to the infirmary to be examined."

"But the manager said that he couldn't feel his pulse, indicating that he might be dead," I protested.

"He'll explain that away by saying that he's not a medical person, and just because he couldn't find a pulse didn't mean there wasn't one. Then he'll give his apologies and say that under the circumstances, the show will not continue, and thank everyone for understanding. Next, he'll ask everyone to vacate the theater. Jasmine, there was nothing we could do, and I wanted to get ahead of the crowd."

I heard voices and turned to see others coming from the theater.

"Come on," said Steve. "Let's go to the piano lounge and get a drink before everyone else gets there."

It was still a little early for the pianist, so there were plenty of places to sit. We sat toward the back in two chairs by a small cocktail table. I prefer to sit closer to the piano player, but this particular night I was fine sitting where we did.

After asking me what I'd like, Steve ordered two glasses of Chardonnay. I must have looked frazzled because he kept telling me to relax and take deep breaths.

"Do you think it was a medical condition?" I asked.

"It appears so," said Steve. "What else could it be?"

I took a sip of my wine and leaned back in the chair. "Maybe he was poisoned, and maybe that's what happened to the first victim."

"Not likely."

"Why?"

"Couple of reasons. For one, he was perfectly fine the whole time he was singing until he fell and went into convulsions. Poison usually doesn't work that way—it's much slower—at least what little I know of it. Secondly, the culprit knows they're looking for him, and if he was hoping to make his victim's death look like an accident . . . well, he failed. Why risk it when he can get off in Honolulu and not return to the ship? And what possible motive would he have for killing the singer? I think he had a reason for killing the first victim." I had to admit that Steve made some valid points.

The piano player had just begun his first number when I started feeling lightheaded. I looked down at my glass and it was empty. I usually don't feel lightheaded after one glass of wine—although I did have wine this afternoon in the Piazza, but that was hours ago.

"Steve, I'm not feeling so good. It could just be stress and anxiety about everything that's been happening, but my equilibrium seems off. I don't think it's from the wine, but it has been a long day, so I'm going to call it a night and head back to my room. Thank you for the company and the wine."

"I'll get our server and settle the tab, then I'll walk with you to make sure you get there safely."

"I appreciate the offer, but it's not necessary. I'm sure I'll be fine," I said. When I stood up to leave, I noticed the man from the elevator sitting on the other side of the room. He wasn't looking at me, but just his presence made me uncomfortable, and I was feeling woozy. "On second thought, Steve, I think I'll take you up on your offer. I don't seem to be very steady right now." I didn't mention seeing the man from the elevator.

By the time we got to the fourteenth floor, I was very glad to have Steve with me because I could barely walk straight. I'm sure if anyone saw me, they would assume I was drunk. Steve held onto my arm.

"This is ridiculous!" I stammered. "I've never had this kind of reaction to alcohol."

"It happens," said Steve. "There's been a lot going on, and if I'm to be honest, I'm feeling a little anxious. It's probably a combination of things, and it has been a long day. Hopefully, when you get in the room and can lie down, you'll feel better."

Steve followed me in my room and I sat down on the edge of the bed. "Thank you for the assistance," I said. "You can leave now. I really don't need a babysitter or a caretaker. I'll be fine." I started to get up and walk him to the door, but my legs felt like they didn't want to move. "I think you'll have to let yourself out. I need to lay down before I pass out." I expected Steve to leave but instead, he sat in the chair by the sliding doors.

"I'm not going anywhere," he said.

"Please don't stay. I really want you to leave," I said, still sitting on the edge of the bed.

"Jasmine, are you worried about cabin 354, and that the same thing might happen to you?"

"How do you know about cabin 354? I never mentioned it to you or to anyone."

"Then you do know something happened in that room."

"I saw them wheeling a person out on a gurney, but I don't know what happened. Do you?" All of a sudden it hit me. "You're not a journalist, are you?"

"I was an employed journalist until I got fired—which I won't go into. Since then, I've been freelancing articles to different newspapers and magazines. Some bite and some don't, so it doesn't pay well. I never thought about it until it happened to me, but when you're used to a certain lifestyle and then lose it, it's amazing what you'll do when you're desperate."

"Was it a man or a woman that was killed in cabin 354?" I was beginning to feel worse and laid back on the pillow. I knew then that I'd been drugged.

"A man."

"Why did you kill him?" At this point I felt like everything was going in slow motion, and I was still trying to understand what was happening.

"A while back, I wrote an article about this pickpocket, Bryan. It turned out to be one of the best stories I've covered, and I learned a lot about the trade. Bryan showed me a lot of tricks on how to take something from someone without them knowing. At the time I found it interesting, but I never anticipated how useful and helpful it would become, until I became unemployed. I thought a cruise would be a good place to try it out. I took a cruise last month and it proved successful. There's a lot of people coming and going, thinking about what they're going to do next, and they don't even realize that they're missing a necklace or watch until hours later. Getting back to your question, I didn't plan to kill him, I just wanted his very expensive Rolex watch. The problem was, he caught me taking it. I told him I saw it falling from his wrist and caught it just in time. He was skeptical, but he had no proof that I was trying to steal it, and I look pretty honest. I offered to buy him a drink and, of course, I slipped something in his cocktail."

My head was fuzzy, and now I felt like I couldn't move my arms. I didn't know how much time I had left, and I wanted to know everything. "Did you help him to his cabin? It won't be long before they figure out who you are. The ship has cameras."

"No, I didn't need to help him. I only gave him enough to make him feel that something wasn't right so he'd go back to his room. I told him I'd have a cabin steward stop by and check on him."

By this point, my vision was blurred and Steve's face looked distorted. "I take it that you were the cabin steward?"

"Very good, Jasmine. Before going to his room, I changed clothes, then put on a fake mustache and glasses in the restroom outside the theater. I knew I'd be off the ship and long gone if they discovered who I was, but I really didn't think they'd suspect foul play."

I could tell my speech was slurred. "How much time do I have before I'm no longer conscious?"

"About thirty minutes. It will take a few more hours before you die, but you'll be in a coma and you won't feel anything. I have to say, Jasmine, I really like you and I'm going to miss you."

"You won't get away with it. We have another full day before docking in Honolulu. My cabin steward will find me in the morning, and the cameras will show you as the last person in my room."

"I thought about that," Steve said. "I'm leaving a Please Don't Disturb card on your doorknob, stating that you have a terrible migraine and request privacy until time to disembark, or until the note has been removed. I've heard that the authorities will be going floor to floor questioning people before allowing them to depart the ship in Honolulu. I'm on the ninth floor and you're on the fourteenth, so it will be a while before they find you. It should look like you died from natural causes—probably cardiac arrest."

I was finding it more difficult to talk, but there was one more thing I had to know. "Why me? I'm not rich, and you won't find a lot of money in my cabin."

"When I walked into the piano lounge, looking for a place to sit," Steve began, "I couldn't help but notice your rings—I knew I had to meet you. You obviously have no concept of their value or you wouldn't be wearing all of them at once, especially on a cruise ship. But I suppose one doesn't expect to get robbed on a ship. I have a good 'fence' and he can get enough for those rings to support my lifestyle for the next month or two. And with the Rolex watch, I should be okay for a while. I'll lay low from cruising in the meantime. Maybe I'll take the train next. I don't think they'll consider foul play in your case, and once they perform an autopsy on the guy in 354, the coroner should rule cause of death undetermined or, at best, cardiac arrest."

I could feel myself slipping away and I didn't think I could talk anymore. I was falling in and out of consciousness. At one point, I thought I felt Steve taking the rings off my hands, but I knew there was nothing I could do about it—I couldn't move. The last thing I remember was a loud sound, then voices, then no more.

I woke up in a hospital bed in Honolulu, and my parents were sitting next to me. My mother and father were listed as my emergency contacts, and by the time the ship arrived in Honolulu, they were already there anxiously waiting. My mother was allowed to ride in the ambulance with me, and my father followed in the rental car. The doctors weren't sure if I'd survive and said as much to my parents. This, of course, I didn't know until I came out of the coma, which I'd been in for almost three days. Once I could grasp where I was and why, I had no end of questions. My parents began explaining what was told to them.

After the man in cabin 354 mysteriously died, security reviewed the passenger list. Steve's name rose to the top of their narrow list of "persons of interest" because he was the only one who'd been on their sister ship the month before where many passengers reported valuable items missing, lost, or possibly stolen. Then when Steve and I were in the lounge, the waitperson who served our wine thought he saw Steve put something in my glass. He wasn't sure at first, but knowing I seemed fine when he brought the wine, he became concerned after observing the difficulty I was having when I got up to leave. Something didn't seem right to him, so he reported it.

In the midst of telling me all this, we were interrupted when someone entered the room.

"Hello, Ms. Jasmine. It's good to see you're awake."

I couldn't believe my eyes. Standing next to my bed was the tattooed man from the elevator. "Who are you? And why are you here?" I asked.

He smiled. "I'm Bruce Atkins, and I'm a bounty hunter."

"A bounty hunter?"

"Yes, but that's not why I was on the ship. My wife and I were long overdue for a vacation, so we booked a cruise to Hawaii. I stopped by yesterday, but you were still in a coma." I looked at my mother.

"I didn't have time to get to that part," she said. "I did meet Bruce when he came by yesterday, and he gave me more information, but I'll let him tell you."

I was still confused and turned my attention to Bruce. He grabbed a chair and sat down. I asked my father to raise the bed so I could see him better. "Why would you have information about what happened to me?" I asked.

"When I'm not looking for someone who skipped bail or was otherwise on the run from the law, I help my brother in his private investigating agency. After the Captain made the announcement that it looked like foul play in the death of a passenger, to my wife's chagrin I offered my services."

Bruce Atkins had my attention and I wanted to hear more. "Do you remember being in the elevator with me?" I asked.

"Yes. It's difficult for someone who looks like me to go unnoticed, so trying to spy on someone discreetly can be challenging. I was asked to observe Steve, and the people he was with. At the time, I didn't know how connected you were to him, and I thought if I ignored you, you'd brush it off and not pay any attention to me if Steve was with you."

"So that's why you were in the lounge when he poisoned me."

"I didn't know if you saw me, so I only glanced your direction every so often. I didn't see Steve put anything in your glass. A few minutes after you got up to leave, your server came over and told me what he thought he saw. I alerted security and we formed a task force, including the ship's doctor who'd been informed that this could be a poisoning. Once we were organized, we were told to meet at your cabin and someone would be there with a key. When you didn't answer the door, we let ourselves in. While the doctor was attending to you, we were questioning Steve, and another member of the task force was searching his room—where he found more poison."

The nurse came in with a glass of water and pills. When I reached for them, I noticed my rings were gone. "He took my rings!"

Bruce searched his pocket and pulled out a Ziplock bag containing my rings. "You might want to let your mother hold onto these until you're ready to leave the hospital." I smiled, and my mother put my rings in her purse.

When I was ready to be discharged, the doctor came in and gave me a clean bill of health. He said surviving the poisoning was a miracle in itself, but I was also fortunate not to have any physical side effects. I certainly have fodder for my next book—should I choose to write about it.

Three months have passed since my return home, and I'm doing pretty well considering. I learned that the singer from the theater had a seizure during his performance, but . . . he's since recovered and is back doing what he loves.

Steve was arrested and charged with murder in the death of the man in cabin 354 and attempted murder on my life. And with my eyewitness account, Steve will never have another opportunity to practice his newfound craft—that of a pickpocket murderer.

The cruise line was wonderful to work with and even paid my out-of-pocket medical expenses. And since I didn't have a chance to complete my cruise, they offered me a complimentary ten-day cruise in an upgraded balcony suite to a destination of my choice. At first, I questioned whether or not I'd want go but, seriously, what are the chances of lightning striking twice?

I decided to accept their offer. I leave in three weeks for Panama, but this time, my rings won't be going with me—well, maybe just one.

Freeda

Freeda attending her grandson's wedding in Cheyenne. She is 94.

FREEDA

I first met Freeda
Shoveling snow from her driveway
She was ninety-one at the time
I soon discovered there was much
To admire about Freeda,
Independent, self-reliant
Loves to dance, cook, and socialize
In her well-kept home
Where she lives alone
If you are in the neighborhood
Knock on her door
You won't need an invitation
A smile will welcome you in
If not at home
She may be at lunch
Or dinner, sitting at the bar
Enjoying conversations
From one end to the other
Now at ninety-five
Freeda still drives, lives alone, cooks
Keeps an immaculate house
Without outside help
An inspiration for us all

FREEDA

I first met Freeda when she was ninety-one, although I didn't know that was her age at the time. She was shoveling her driveway and I was returning home from an appointment. I stopped to ask if I could help. When I rolled my window down, I was hit with a blast of cold air. Freeda walked up to the car.

"It's really cold out here," I said after introducing myself. "Would you like some help?"

"Oh, no," she replied. "I'm almost through."

I looked up at my driveway, which was still covered with an inch and a half of snow, and then I looked at Freeda. "I was hoping the sun would melt it by this afternoon so I wouldn't have to shovel, but I guess it's too cold for that."

"Well, I don't think that's going to happen, and we face north. It's also wet and heavy," she added.

After pulling the car into the garage, I decided to clear my driveway. Freeda was right, it was wet and heavy and the air was bitter cold. I could only get a few feet done at a time before having to go inside to warm up. I wanted to quit, but when I looked down the street at Freeda's clean driveway and sidewalk, I was motivated to keep going. I thought about how she seemed to clear it so effortlessly, yet I struggled, and I was almost two decades younger than she. I wondered if Freeda had to go inside to warm up and rest in between shoveling as I did. When I stopped to talk to her, she wasn't even out of breath. She had a vitality and spirit that I was drawn to, and I knew at that moment that I wanted to know more about this woman named Freeda.

Two years would pass before I'd have another opportunity to meet up again with Freeda. Part of it had to do with lingering Covid outbreaks and not getting out much. I also never seemed to see her when I'd walk down to get my mail.

One day I ran into my neighbor, Claudia, at the mailbox. She lives next door to Freeda and two doors down from me. We started chatting and I asked her if she saw much of Freeda.

"Yes, we go to lunch once in a while. Last year I took her out for her birthday, but this year I was out of town so she took herself to dinner and celebrated her ninety-third birthday. She told me that she sat at the bar because she enjoys the company of others and doesn't like sitting at a table alone. She has no problem talking to strangers."

"I've only met her once, but she was friendly. It's a shame she didn't have someone to take her to dinner and celebrate her birthday with her."

"Well, here's the funny part," Claudia said. "When her check never came, she asked the bartender for it, and he replied that she didn't owe anything. He told her that one customer paid for her dinner and another paid for her drinks."

I shook my head and smiled. I was impressed. "I don't know if I would have the courage, or stamina for that matter, at ninety-three to do what Freeda did," I said. "Claudia, I would love to visit with Freeda. She sounds like an amazing woman and someone I'd enjoy knowing."

"She is amazing," said Claudia. "She's very independent, lives by herself, does her own cleaning, and enjoys cooking. She drives herself everywhere she wants to go—shopping, going out to eat, and visiting friends. Since you want to meet her, I'll have you and Freeda and some of the other neighbors over one evening, and you can visit with her." I thanked Claudia and we each went our respective ways.

A week later at Claudia's house—and before the other guests arrived—I found myself talking endlessly with Freeda. At five feet tall, this petite ninety-three-year-old with good posture had a zest for life that far too many people years younger seemed to have lost. She had a sparkle in her eye, and I could tell that she enjoyed talking and being around people. I was sure she'd done a lot of entertaining in her day, and probably still did.

Later that night as I was getting ready for bed, I couldn't stop thinking about Freeda and the many things she shared with me during our conversation. Her first job—other than babysitting—was with the State of Wyoming Highway Department. She was eighteen and had just graduated from high school. On July 1, 1947, Wyoming passed the first driver's license law, and Freeda was the person who issued the very first license. Before that time, anyone could get behind the wheel of a car and drive. Once the law passed, kids eighteen and nineteen would lie about their age and claim to be twenty-one so they'd be of legal age to drink. Nobody questioned them, and even though Freeda knew they weren't that age, she was told to go by what they had put down on their application.

I thought all of that was interesting, but it was what she told me next that really piqued my interest. Freeda loves to dance. On her eighty-fifth birthday, she was living in Cheyenne, Wyoming, and her grandchildren had a birthday party for her at Alf's Pub. They turned the candles on the cake to read 58 instead of 85. Someone dared her to get up on the table and dance, so she did. Now . . . I enjoy dancing, but I couldn't imagine getting up on a table at my age, let alone eighty-five! There was a prideful gleam in her eye as she related the story. And to be honest, I felt a little envious.

That evening was the beginning of many visits with Freeda. We'd either get together at her house, Claudia's, or mine. And usually there'd be food and wine. The three of us also enjoyed going out to lunch once in a while. On Freeda's ninety-fourth birthday, Claudia and I took her to lunch. By this time, I'd learned a lot about her. I believe it was during this three-hour lunch when I first realized that I wanted to write about her. I was fascinated by her energy, stamina, positive attitude, and love for life—which seemed to be the catalyst that propelled her to a century. I hope by telling her story, and sharing some of her incredible adventures, that it will inspire others to enjoy life to the fullest, as Freeda has inspired me to do.

As I continued my conversations with Freeda, I learned more about her childhood and early adult years, and I began to understand why she kept such a positive attitude even during difficult times. It just wasn't her style to let anything get her down. I wish I had an answer for why some people are able to do this and others aren't, but I don't. I do believe that if we see the glass half full rather than half empty, it might make it a little easier to maneuver the curves life throws at us.

Freeda Mae Self was born in Paxton, Nebraska, on April 15, 1929, to Vera M. Cornick and Lewis Edwards Self. Lewis worked for Union Pacific as a section foreman in Wyoming. He was in Nebraska to repair tracks with his extra gang who lived in the train bunk cars while repairing the tracks. They'd work on one section then move on to the next, either repairing or laying new tracks. At the time, Vera and Lewis had been married for two years and Vera was pregnant with their first child, Freeda. The family moved back to Wyoming when Freeda was between two and three months old. Lewis continued working on the railroad tracks in Wyoming with the section hands—also called gandy dancers—who worked for him.

Vera was eighteen when Freeda was born. She'd always had Lewis to herself, but with the arrival of their firstborn, Lewis began shifting more of his attention to the baby. He doted on Freeda. The more attention he gave to her the less he gave to Vera, and it wasn't long before Vera became resentful of their relationship. As Freeda grew, so did the closeness with her father, and so did Vera's resentment. Vera wasn't abusive to Freeda, but she was never loving towards her either. There were times she'd send her off to live with relatives just to get her out of the house and away from Lewis. But as the family grew, Freeda was brought back home when Vera needed help with the younger children. Although Freeda received very little attention from her mother, it was showered on her younger brother and sister. Her brother, Frank, was his mother's favorite, and Vera loved him dearly. Frank and her sister, Shirley, never had to do anything around the house. It was Freeda's job to do all the chores—Shirley never even made her own bed, Freeda did. She must have felt like Cinderella . . . if only she'd had a fairy godmother.

Freeda did have some positive memorable moments during her childhood, and one was playing the piano. A husband and wife gave lessons and turned part of their very large home into a music conservatory. Freeda started taking lessons at the age of thirteen. She didn't own a piano, but the couple allowed her to use theirs. Every day, she'd walk ten blocks to their house to practice. She did this right up through high school. She loved classical music and studied Bach and Beethoven. It didn't come easy for her, but she worked hard and became very good at her craft. She took lessons on an eight-foot baby grand piano and when she got better, she was promoted to the grand piano at the age of fifteen. At her school recital, Freeda performed a dual piano piece with her teacher on the grand piano and won. She aspired to be a concert pianist, but during her senior year, a friend introduced her to Wayland Warren. He had just come home from World War Two and Freeda fell hard for him. After graduation, at the age of eighteen, Freeda and Wayland married, and that ended her music career.

They were married in 1947, but they eventually grew apart and divorced in 1969. Freeda was blessed with two sons and the grandchildren that she'd always hoped to have.

During her life, Freeda held many jobs and was very good at all of them. In 1977, she was living in Arizona when she learned that her father was very ill. One day when I was visiting with her, I asked her to tell me about her time in Arizona and her father's illness.

"I was living in Phoenix at the time. I was with the Wild Women of the West, doing my thing—riding horses, working with Angels Handy Dan as their corporate accountant, and just enjoying life when I learned that my father was diagnosed with terminal cancer."

"What is Angels Handy Dan?" I asked.

"It's a do-it-yourself store similar to Lowe's. I paid out everything that came in for the store. I did that for four stores in Arizona."

"Were you able to take time off to be with your father? Was he still living in Wyoming?"

"Yes, he was in Wyoming. I went home at Christmastime and my brother came from Texas—that's where he was living at the time. I told my boss that I was up and down and didn't know what to do or how long I'd have to be gone. He was very understanding and told me to do what I had to do, and they would have someone fill in for me."

I thought about how much Freeda's dad loved her. Vera never showed her love, she just seemed to tolerate her, but Freeda could always count on her dad to make her feel loved.

"That had to be a very difficult time for you," I said.

"It was. Dad was not doing well. Frank and I talked about many different things. He worked at Stern Rogers on the power plant, and he was moving to Craig, Colorado because Stern Rogers was building one there. Frank said to me, 'Sis, why don't you come to Craig with me and work at the power plant instead of going back to Phoenix? We'll be closer to Dad and can go home every weekend.' So, I applied for a job with Stern Rogers. They didn't hire related people at the time, but we had different last names so we covered it up."

"That's right, I'd forgotten that you were divorced by this time."

"Oh, yes, I'd been divorced for quite a while by then."

"Did you get the job?"

"Yes, I did. I got the job in accounts payable because of my experience in Phoenix. But due to lack of housing, I lived with my brother and sister-in-law. People at work thought it was great—Frank had two wives—ha ha! Our site supervisor was Vern, and he was a really nice guy. I'd have to go down to Denver with Vern occasionally to the main office. The company had a plane that we'd fly on from Craig to Denver. Well, Vern's mother lived in Denver and we'd stay at her house when we went. Here's the funny part about that—she'd put me at one end of the house and Vern at the other end, because she didn't want us getting together. Little did she know that her son was gay."

"Oh, that's funny!" I said. We both laughed.

"I was no more than a buddy to him, but I guess she thought otherwise and was determined to keep us separated. Vern asked if it bothered me, and I told him no, I thought it was hilarious! I would never let on and I'd play her little game."

"Did you visit your father on the weekends?"

"Yes. My father was failing and the doctors said that he needed to go to a nursing home."

"Did he go to the nursing home?" I asked.

"No. My mother, brother, and sister got together and discussed what should be done. I wasn't included in the conversation. They decided—without consulting me—that Dad would not go into a nursing home. Instead, I would quit my job—that I'd grown to love—and move to Wyoming. Needless to say, I was not happy with the decision. And yet, I wanted to take care of my dad. I was upset with the way it was done. My life was turned upside down and I wasn't even included in the discussion."

"Oh, Freeda, that had to be very hard on you. How did you support yourself?"

"It was a full-time job, and I had no income. Frank would give me $100 one month and Shirley did the same the next month, so at least I had money for personal items. But they never helped with his care."

"Did your mother help any?"

"Mother's health wasn't the best at that time—she had Parkinson's—and she only made things worse."

"How so?"

"I guess she was angry that he was dying and her mean streak came out. Every time she went past him, she would pinch and hit him when he didn't seem to do what she wanted him to do. Dad would cry, and that's why he turned night and day upside down. He was so sick, and to avoid her attacks, he would sleep during the day when my mother was up, and stay up all night. I would stay up with him and try to catch a few cat naps during the day, but it was difficult."

"Did you have any down time?"

"There were some fun times, mostly having happy hour at our place on Friday nights. It filled in for not being able to go anywhere or do anything. Mom and Dad sold their property and they were living in an apartment at that time. So, on Friday nights we'd invite the neighbors in for hors d'oeuvres, wine, and cocktails. Mom was a beer drinker and we'd have beer for her.

My sister would come over occasionally and sit for a few hours so I could get out and run some errands. She didn't do this often because she had issues of her own and wasn't always capable. But it turned out pretty well. Then after Dad passed, I went back to Phoenix in 1978 and I rejoined the Wild Women of the West and settled into my life again."

I had never heard of the Wild Women of the West, but it was obviously something Freeda enjoyed being a part of, so I wanted to know more.

"Freeda, what exactly is the Wild Women of the West?"

She smiled, "I'll give you the gist of it now, but I have a sheet of paper that was given to me at our twenty-year reunion that explains how the organization got started and what they did and the qualifications to join. I think it was written by one of the original members. Anyway, they were a group of women who started out to portray outlaw women of the West—women like Annie Oakley, Poker Face Alice, Big Nose Kate, etc. They started out as a riding group and rode in parades. We had covers over the horses that said 'Wild Women of the West,' and we dressed the part. We were pretty well-known around the Phoenix area, and we'd go to Tombstone and places like that."

"Was it fun to be known as 'wild women'?" I teased.

"Yes, it was a lot of fun. We traveled around to a lot of places, and that's when I was in Prescott for the very first time. We rode in the rodeo and we rode in the parade, and that's where I got thrown from the horse. I was hurt pretty bad. But I got up and walked away," she laughed.

"I'm not surprised," I said shaking my head.

"I was a tough cookie!"

"Yes, I think you were." We both laughed.

I'm not sure when I got the sheet of paper from Freeda explaining the Wild Women of the West, but I found it interesting and wanted to include it.

How it all started:

A woman by the name of Dorothy Dalguard had a basic but sound idea that she believed in. She knew if she could find the right bunch of women she could form an organization that would be interesting, fun, and also dedicated to pre-serving the memory of the women who helped make the west famous.

The group started in 1973 with 5 women, Dorothy Dalguard, Babs Grant, Penny Simpson, Lynn Ashly, and Ammie Commie. They decided to start the famous Wild Women of the West. The qualifications to be a Wild Women of the West were; you had to be single and own a horse. Rumor has it that initiation included riding your horse up a mountain {hill} with a can of beer in hand. You were allowed two drinks prior to taking your ride. Then up the hill you went as fast as you could go and then back down again. The object was not to spill any of your beer. Then off you rode into an old bar on Bell road—this is when there was nothing out there—where you rode in and took a shot, your choice, then out you went . . . hoping your horse didn't leave a present.

Dorothy was the only one at the time who didn't portray an actual person. She played an Indian by the name of Princess Morning Star. Their trappings started out with blue satin and white lettering with white fringe across the bottom.

Each new member must complete a six-month qualification time, research her character and give a report at the end of her qualification period. You still needed to own a horse, but you can be hitched or single. Each member must know her chatter well and dress as authentically as possible with her costume relating directly to her character's reputation or profession.

The Wild Women of the West have come a long way. Now you see them in their glory with their yellow and black trappings going down the parade route creating a ruckus. Membership is limited to 25. We do parades throughout Arizona as well as out of state. Other activities include lectures and appearance at schools, historical societies, rodeo grand entries, sneak movie premieres and festivals. This group takes pride in its civic involvement as well as assisting other endeavors such as, sponsoring fundraisers for other non-profit organizations.

As of ten years ago the group was still in existence, but as of this writing, Freeda hasn't been in touch so she's not sure what they might be up to. Freeda was always on the move. She'd be in Phoenix for a while, then Jackson, Wyoming, and then back to Cheyenne to help take care of her grandchildren. She returned to Phoenix for the tenth anniversary of the Wild Women of the West, then again for their twentieth anniversary.

Freeda, Claudia, and I go to lunch or meet at each other's houses more often now, and our friendships continue to grow. Each time Claudia and I engage in conversation with Freeda, I'm learning there's still so much more that I don't know about her. But considering I'm delving into almost one hundred years of someone's life and all the history she's lived through, I realize that it's going to take more than a few lunches and get-togethers to uncover it all.

On this particular day in August of 2023, Freeda and I took Claudia to lunch for her birthday. Out of the blue, Freeda started talking about a harrowing experience she had at hunting camp while she was still living in Jackson before moving to Cheyenne.

"Did you used to go hunting?" I asked in disbelief.

"Oh, no," she said, "I was the cook for the hunters."

Just for the record, I have almost six pages of notes leading up to how Freeda became the cook at hunting camp. But given that this is a short story, I will have to save that information for her full-length biography.

Claudia was as eager to hear about the experience at hunting camp as I was, but first, I wanted to understand what the setup was like for a hunting camp and exactly what she was expected to do.

"Freeda, where was hunting camp, and what was it like?"

"You leave Jackson, Wyoming, and go towards Colter Bay, which is only a few miles from the southeast corner of Yellowstone Park," she began. "Then you get off the highway onto a dirt road for five miles to base camp. That's as far as you can go by car. Base camp is where you'd pick up the horses, mules, and supplies. The mules were needed to carry the supplies. We'd continue on horseback fifteen to eighteen miles through steep and difficult terrain to Brown Meadow where the hunting camp was. In one area, we'd go over a hill and down into a beautiful meadow where there would be elk. You had to be very quiet or the elk would charge you. When we left the meadow and went over the mountain, the topography changed into a cliffhanger—a very narrow trail about three to four feet wide with quite a drop off. It seemed like we endured this for one to two miles. One time we lost a pack mule weighed down with supplies when he was either spooked or lost his footing and went over the cliff."

"That sounds awful! I probably would've given up when I got to base camp," I said. "Freeda, I'm just not as adventurous as you are. How long did it take you to get to the hunting camp?"

"Based on what I remember, it was between five and six hours."

"What was it like when you got there?"

"There were two men to each tent. I had my own tent with my dog, John Wesley Hardin. I called him J.W. I also had a camp jack—he was a young boy. Our job was to see that the tents had water, firewood, fire starter for the stoves, and to make sure the lanterns were full."

"So, his job was to help you. Did he stay with you during the day while the men went hunting?" I asked.

"Yes, but he was young. I think it was during the second hunt when he went to town and never came back."

I laughed. "Smart kid."

"They didn't know he wasn't going to come back, and I didn't have a camp jack anymore."

"Did you do it all by yourself?"

"Yes, I did."

"What 'all' did you have to do?"

"The guides went up the week before I did to set up camp. They set up the tents for the hunters and the cook tent. Then they came back for me and the supplies. They had everything set up when I got there, which was right after Labor Day. Some of the guides brought the hunters in the next day. They had to bring hunters and supplies in every three to four days, depending on the hunt that had been bought. My job, in addition to keeping the tents supplied, was to make sure that there was coffee by daylight. Then I'd cook breakfast for everyone. There were four to five guides, the camp jack—while he was there, and four to six hunters at a time. I fixed lunch for those who stayed and packed a lunch for those who went hunting, and I'd have dinner for them at night. I was busy cooking and cleaning up all day," she explained.

"Freeda, did you ever feel uneasy, or did anything ever happen to concern you about being the only woman with all those men in a remote area?"

"No. I knew how to take care of myself, and I had my dog. Besides, those men were all gentlemen and they paid a lot of money for that trip. It wasn't cheap."

"So, what was the harrowing experience, and when did it happen?"

"The last night at hunting camp," she said. "I don't think I've ever been that frightened." We'd finished our lunch, so Freeda had our full attention. "That morning, I fixed breakfast for the hunters and they left early. We started breaking down camp and the guides were getting ready to pack up and load the mules—which takes a while—when it began to snow. I was cleaning up and came across a bottle of vodka. I showed it to the guides and, instead of continuing to pack up so we could get out of there by noon, we decided to make drinks with the leftover Kool-Aid. While we procrastinated, enjoying our drinks, the snowfall became heavier and heavier and the

Freeda and J.W. at the hunting camp.

ground was covered. The guides decided they'd better get back to loading the mules. After a while, one of the guides came over to tell me that I'd better pack up and start back to base camp before it got dark. He said it would be at least a couple more hours before they were ready to leave. He told me to take one of the mules because it would be steadier and safer in this weather than a horse. In addition to my mule, I had four other loaded-down pack mules going with me and my husky, J.W. It was so cold. The snow was getting deep, and I had almost eighteen miles to go and dusk was approaching. I was on my own. Not only was I cold but I was scared, and I felt responsible for getting the mules to base camp without harm. Mules are smart: They knew the trail, but at night in that kind of weather, anything could happen."

"What time of year was it?" I asked.

"November, a couple of weeks before Thanksgiving. I had been there since right after Labor Day. I think it was at this point when I realized why the hunters were shocked to see this petite woman at hunting camp. And I began to understand why it was so hard to get someone to be the cook and do what I did. When I volunteered for the job, I thought it would be like base camp—I'd have a cabin and a kitchen, not a tent and cooking outside on a grate over a fire. I really had no idea what I was getting myself into. I'm glad I did it, but after that last night, I would never do it again."

"How much daylight did you have before it got dark? Were you able to get over the cliffhanger before nightfall?"

"Yes. That area was about a third of the way down and it wasn't completely dark yet. I was glad to make it through there because the weather wasn't letting up. It had snowed off and on most of the time I had been at camp, so there was already a lot of snow. About halfway down, I was freezing and my gloves and boots weren't much help. I wanted to get off my mule so I could get some circulation going, but the snow was up to the mule's belly. I was concerned that if I got off, I wouldn't be able to get back on, and the mules would wander off without me. I've never been afraid of anything most of my life—I was a daredevil. This was the first time that I can remember feeling that frightened. I was so focused on making sure that I got to camp safely and didn't fall asleep that I don't remember thinking about anything else. It took hours, but I made it."

"What happened when you got to base camp?"

"I was stiff and I couldn't move. The guys came out and helped me off the mule. My hands and toes were frostbitten. They took me inside, rubbed my hands, and gave me some brandy."

Freeda, shortly before hunting camp.

There were many daredevil and humorous stories that Freeda shared over the course of a few years. But just when I thought I knew everything there was to know about her, she surprised me with an adventure she had that I'm sure most eighty-seven-year-old women would never even consider. Not only did she consider it, she never thought of it as being unusual.

"Freeda, if you were eighty-seven, this must have been in 2017," I said.

"Yes, it was July 2017. I was invited to go four-wheeling in Wycolo, Wyoming, to celebrate my friend Bobbie's birthday. She had a cabin there and she said several of our other friends would be joining us. It sounded like a lot of fun to me and I jumped at the chance."

At that age it didn't sound like a lot of fun to me, but then I wasn't Freeda. "Did you fly to Cheyenne?" I asked.

"No, I drove from Prescott—where I was living at the time—to Wycolo. I had no problem driving."

I had this visual of elderly people going four-wheeling and—being in my seventies—I couldn't even imagine such a thing. "How many friends were there, and were they all about your age?"

"No, they were in their early forties. There were six women and seven men. Not all were in the same cabin, but we had a lot of the get-togethers at Bobbie's. I stayed with Raylene and her husband, Ron, in their cabin."

"And you all went four-wheeling?"

"Oh, yes! It was so much fun! I have to tell you a funny thing that happened to me while we were on the trail. Well, it wasn't funny at the time, but I find it amusing now. We had been riding on the trails through the woods and decided to stop so we could stretch and take a potty break. Everyone ran into the woods to do their thing. I thought I'd found a great spot so I dropped my pants down to my ankles and held onto a low-lying branch in case I needed help getting up. I didn't realize how difficult it would be to squat at eighty-seven and keep your balance. Well, I started to fall and so I held tight to the branch, but it wasn't very strong and it broke off," she giggled.

"Oh, my gosh! What happened?"

"I fell backwards with my feet over my head and my butt in the air. I couldn't get up so I yelled for Raylene to come help me. I must have sounded like I was being attacked by some wild animal, because not only did Raylene come running, but so did everyone else—including the men!"

"What did you do? You must have been so embarrassed."

"I looked at the guys and said, 'If you haven't seen a butt before, you're seeing one now.' If I was embarrassed, I didn't stay that way. I was glad for the help and I wasn't going to let that spoil my fun."

My friendship with Freeda has been one of the highlights of my life. I don't think I've ever met anyone who's enjoyed life as much as she has—and still does. No matter what emotional turmoil she may have gone through with her mother, it seemed to make her stronger and appreciate life even more.

In 1990, Freeda was still living in Cheyenne and so was her mother. Vera became very ill with cancer and was undergoing radiation. Freeda was working with the State of Wyoming Port of Entry as a supervisor.

"Frank would take Mother for radiation and I would stay with her after her treatment. If she was too bad for me to leave her the next morning, then I'd have to call work and let them know that I wouldn't be there. Frank helped when he could, but there's only so much a man can do. I bathed Mother, did her hair, and cooked for her—things like that."

"How was your mother's behavior toward you during this time?"

"Oh, she had her moments. One time when I cooked dinner, she didn't think I'd cooked it right and threw a plate of peas at me. She always told me that I couldn't do anything right, no matter how hard I tried."

"That had to be difficult since you were taking care of her and doing the best you could."

"I knew how sick she was and I tried not to let it get to me."

"Do you think in the end that she really did appreciate you?"

"I don't know. The night she died, I was combing her hair and she looked at me and said, 'Freeda, I don't know what I would have done without you,' but she never told me that she loved me."

After all these years, sharing this brought tears to Freeda's eyes and I could see the hurt that she must've endured. "It's still painful that your mother never said, 'I love you,' isn't it?" She nodded and looked at me.

"But you know what?" she said. "Just having her say what she did erased a lot of resentment that I had towards her."

Freeda continues to inspire me on a daily basis. Her strength, determination, independent spirit, and love for life is never taken for granted. She is thankful for every God-given day, and she enjoys every minute of it.

I wish I could share all the wonderful highlights of Freeda's life, but it would be impossible to do so in a mini-bio. So, I'll finish with some meaningful and special moments in condensed versions—along with pictures—of this extraordinary woman as she looks forward to becoming a vivacious centenarian.

One of the most memorable and rewarding times in Freeda's life was her volunteer work with the American Legion. Women usually worked the auxiliary side because, in order to be with the honor guard, you had to be military—past or present. She started volunteering with the auxiliary while she was still working. When she retired at sixty-five, she volunteered full time with the American

Legion until she was eighty-five, most of the time working eight to ten hours a day, six days a week, and loving every minute of it.

Freeda accomplished something that no other non-military person had: She became an honorary member of the honor guard. At that time, no one had a pick-up truck but Freeda. The honor guard needed a truck to haul the flags and rifles to the ceremonies, so she offered to do it. After one year of doing this, the honor guard held a meeting and voted to make Freeda an honorary member, even though she wasn't active duty or a veteran. Freeda became chaplain for a couple of years then commander for two years, eventually becoming adjutant. The adjutant helps the commander and is the finance officer.

Before moving to Prescott, Arizona, at the age of eighty-five, Freeda trained someone else to be adjutant. And as adjutant, everything had to be reported to the government. She had mixed emotions when she left because she loved volunteering with the American

FREEDA WARREN

IN APPRECIATION FOR
17 YEARS OF DEDICATED SERVICE
TO THE

AMERICAN LEGION POST #6
HONOR GUARD

Wyoming
Veterans Commission

Certificate of Appreciation
Is Presented To

Ms. Freeda Warren, Post # 6 Honor Guard
Thank you for your outstanding work to provide highly accurate and detailed information regarding the Wyoming Veterans Burial Reimbursement documentation. Your attention to detail and precise documentation has ensured timely payments. Thank you for your outstanding work.

Presented March 11, 2009

Ron Wood
Chairman

Legion, and especially all the work she did with the honor guard. Everyone appreciated and loved Freeda, and she has been greatly missed.

On Freeda's ninetieth birthday, she decided to join forty-two friends from Cheyenne and go to Las Vegas. This was a group that traveled yearly to different places. The friends took the chartered bus from Cheyenne to Denver and then flew to Las Vegas. By this time, Freeda had moved from Prescott to Grand Junction, Colorado, to be near her son and daughter-in-law. She flew from Grand Junction to Las Vegas and met up with her friends. They stayed at the D Casino and Hotel, which was across from the Golden Nugget.

One evening, Freeda and a few of the friends were enjoying drinks and catching up on old times, but Freeda kept being distracted by the girl dancing in the cage. Freeda—known for her love of dance—could hardly sit still. When the girl's shift was over and she left the cage, Freeda told her friends that she wanted to get in there and dance. The friends started daring her to do it. After another drink, and with constant encouragement from her friends, Freeda had mustered up the courage and was ready to go. But just as she was ready to make her move, the pit boss walked by. She stopped him and told him that she wanted to get in the cage and dance. He informed her that if she did, then he'd have to arrest her. She pleaded her case, stating that she really wanted to dance in that cage. Once again, he assured her that if she did, then she would be arrested. It had something to do with the establishment's insurance. The friends dared her to do it anyway, but Freeda gave it some more thought and decided that it wasn't worth going to jail over.

In August of 2023, Freeda—at the age of ninety-four—attended her great-grandson's wedding in Cheynne, Wyoming, which was held outside on a large ranch. It was a beautiful wedding with lots of food and beverages—which she enjoyed tremendously—but what she loved most was the live band and lots of dancing. Freeda's hip had started bothering her around this time, but that didn't stop her from dancing almost every dance for three solid hours.

Claudia and I took Freeda to a restaurant, reminiscent of a speakeasy, to celebrate her ninety-sixth birthday on April 15, 2025. We took a taxi so we wouldn't have to worry about driving home should it be late . . . or for any other reason. Two other friends of Freeda's joined us there and we had a blast!

April 15, 2025 celebrating her 96th birthday.

For two years, Freeda was bothered with her hip. Nothing she did seemed to help and it just kept getting worse. She tried shots, but they only lasted a couple of weeks. She was told that her hip had completely disintegrated and she would need a total hip replacement. Around the time of her ninety-sixth birthday, she started experiencing swelling in her legs. The doctor that she was going to at the time didn't seem to know what was causing the problem and just kept putting her on diuretics. Hip surgery was scheduled for June, but because the swelling in her legs had gotten so bad—causing them to turn purple and creating excruciating pain to the touch—the surgery was postponed. Freeda went to several different specialists, including kidney and pulmonary, and everything checked out fine except with her cardiologist. The cardiologist told her that it was related to her heart. She had heart failure and the only thing keeping her alive was her pacemaker, which was several years old and the battery was running low. She needed a new battery, but first she needed hip surgery so she could walk without pain and get back to the life that she'd always known. After months of being on several different diuretics, some of the swelling lessened, but only slightly.

Freeda was gracious enough to allow Claudia and me to be present at her doctor's appointments. It meant the world to me to be included on this journey with her. And for what it's worth, no matter how much pain she might have been in, we always went to lunch afterwards. She was determined not to completely give in to this debilitating medical setback or to feel sorry for herself—but I'm sure she had her moments. Instead, she wanted to stay focused on what needed to be done to get back to the quality of life she expected.

On November 10, 2025, Freeda finally had her hip surgery. It wasn't performed until early evening so they kept her overnight. It couldn't have gone any better and she was expected to recover fully. Since insurance would not cover staying in rehab, Freeda's granddaughter-in-law, Rachael—who is an RN—took a train from the Front Range to Grand Junction to stay with her for ten days. I went to visit Freeda two days after the surgery and she told me that she had made homemade potato soup for herself and Rachael. I don't know why I was surprised because, after all, it was Freeda. She said since she lived alone, she mainly needed Rachael to make sure she was doing things correctly and not overdoing. I was amazed at how well she was healing and thankful that Rachael was there to keep her in check.

Freeda, two days after hip surgery.

With occasional home physical therapy, Freeda had progressed from the walker to the cane rather quickly. Her cardiologist wanted to schedule having the pacemaker battery replaced on December 17, but Freeda told him that she wasn't quite ready for that yet. He said it had to be done by January 8, or the battery would die. So, on January 7, 2026, Freeda got her new battery. She was wide awake, hungry, and ready to go home when they brought her back from surgery, but they told her she'd have to wait an hour. When the doctor came in, he told Claudia and me that she entertained the operating staff by talking about roasting javelina pigs while living in Arizona.

On our way home, we drove through Culver's so Freeda could get some fish and chips and the three of us got frozen custard. We ate the custard in the parking lot before leaving and Freeda took the fish and chips home to eat later.

Since the beginning of February 2026, Freeda is fully recovered and back to her old self. She is driving, shopping at the mall and doing what she loves—having lunch on Sunday afternoons at Texas Roadhouse, sitting at the bar visiting with old friends and some new. She still enjoys a hug from the young bartender, Cameron, and occasionally—someone without her knowledge—picks up her tab.

Freeda with Cameron, the bartender, and friends that she enjoys when visiting Texas Roadhouse.

Freeda dancing at the Moose two weeks before her 97th birthday.

Freeda's optimism, enthusiasm, and love for socializing, enjoying friends, and meeting new people will live on with everyone who has been blessed to have known her.

Claudia on the left, Debby on the right, celebrating Freeda's 97th birthday.

Happy 97th, Freeda!